The Syntax of Chichewa

This comprehensive study provides a detailed description of the major syntactic structures of Chichewa. Assuming no prior knowledge of current theory, it covers topics such as relative-clause and question formation, interactions between tone and syntactic structure, aspects of clause structure such as complementation, and phonetics and phonology. It also provides a detailed account of argument structure, in which the role of verbal suffixation is examined. Sam Mchombo's description is supplemented by observations about how the study of African languages, specifically Bantu languages, has contributed to progress in grammatical theory, including the debates that have raged within linguistic theory about the relationship between syntax and the lexicon, and the contributions of African linguistic structure to the evaluation of competing grammatical theories. Clearly organized and accessible, *The Syntax of Chichewa* will be an invaluable resource for students interested in linguistic theory and how it can be applied to a specific language.

SAM MCHOMBO is Associate Professor in the Department of Linguistics, University of California at Berkeley. He is possibly the leading authority on Chichewa, having trained other internationally renowned scholars of the language, and inspired a whole generation of students in Malawi with his work on Chichewa poetry. He is well-known and respected both as a language instructor and theoretical linguist, and as well as editing *Theoretical Aspects of Bantu Grammar* (1993), he has published articles in many journals including *Language*, *Linguistic Analysis*, and *Linguistic Inquiry*.

CAMBRIDGE SYNTAX GUIDES

General editors:

P. Austin, J. Bresnan, D. Lightfoot, I. Roberts, N. V. Smith

Responding to the increasing interest in comparative syntax, the goal of the Cambridge Syntax Guides is to make available to all linguists major findings, both descriptive and theoretical, which have emerged from the study of particular languages. The series is not committed to working in any particular framework, but rather seeks to make language-specific research available to theoreticians and practitioners of all persuasions. Written by leading figures in the field, these guides will each include an overview of the grammatical structures of the language concerned. For the descriptivist, the books will provide an accessible introduction to the methods and results of the theoretical literature; for the theoretician, they will show how constructions that have achieved theoretical notoriety fit into the structure of the language as a whole; for everyone, they will promote cross-theoretical and cross-linguistic comparison with respect to a well-defined body of data.

Other books available in this series

O. Fischer et al.:   *The Syntax of Early English*
K. Zagona: *The Syntax of Spanish*
K. Kiss: *The Syntax of Hungarian*

The Syntax of Chichewa

SAM MCHOMBO

PUBLISHED BY THE PRESS SYNDICATE OF THE UNIVERSITY OF CAMBRIDGE
The Pitt Building, Trumpington Street, Cambridge, United Kingdom

CAMBRIDGE UNIVERSITY PRESS
The Edinburgh Building, Cambridge, CB2 2RU, UK
40 West 20th Street, New York, NY 10011–4211, USA
477 Williamstown Road, Port Melbourne, VIC 3207, Australia
Ruiz de Alarcón 13, 28014 Madrid, Spain
Dock House, The Waterfront, Cape Town 8001, South Africa

http://www.cambridge.org

First published 2004

Printed in the United Kingdom at the University Press, Cambridge

Typefaces Times 10/13 pt.   *System* LaTeX 2$_\varepsilon$ [TB]

A catalogue record for this book is available from the British Library

Library of Congress Cataloguing in Publication data

Mchombo, Sam A., 1948–
The syntax of Chichewa / Sam Mchombo.
    p.   cm. – (Cambridge syntax guides)
Includes bibliographical references and index.
ISBN 0 521 57378 5
1. Chewa dialect – Syntax.   I. Title.   II. Series.
PL8110.C51M34   2004
496′.39185 – dc22   2004045633

ISBN 0 521 57378 5 hardback

Dedicated to my mother
Harriett B. Mchombo
who passed away when the book was in production

Contents

7   The verb stem as a domain of linguistic processes   *112*

Acknowledgments

I am deeply indebted to Joan Bresnan for detailed comments on earlier drafts of the manuscript, and for sustained intellectual stimulation over the years. The work would have been infinitely better had I paid attention to all the issues that she raised. I hope that the book has preserved the major points requiring attention and incorporation. I am very grateful to Al Mtenje for prompt and always detailed and cheerful responses to my incessant questions about phonological issues and judgments of Chichewa sentences, and to Thilo Schadeberg for further suggestions for improvement of the manuscript.

Over the years I have been exceptionally fortunate to have had the opportunity to interact with outstanding scholars in African linguistics and linguistic theory. Their influence will be evident on virtually every page of this book. It is a real pleasure to acknowledge their impact on my intellectual development. To this end I express my gratitude to Alex Alsina, Mark Baker, Herman Batibo, Adams Bodomo, Eyamba Bokamba, Robert Botne, Mike Brame, Kunjılıka Chaima, Lisa Cheng, Noam Chomsky, Chris Collins, Mary Dalrymple, Katherine Demuth, Cynthia Zodwa Dlayedwa, Laura Downing, David Dwyer, Joe Emonds, Charles Fillmore, Gregório Firmino, the late Ken Hale, Carolyn Harford, James Higginbotham, Tom Hinnebusch, Leanne Hinton, Larry Hyman, Peter Ihionu, Ray Jackendoff, Jonni Kanerva, Francis Katamba, Paul Kay, Ruth Kempson, Paul Kiparsky, Pascal Kishindo, Nancy Kula, Andrew Tilimbe Kulemeka, George Lakoff, Howard Lasnik, Will Leben, Rose Letsholo, Patricia Mabugu, Victor Manfredi, Lutz Marten, Francis Matambirofa, Sozinho Matsinhe, Sheila Mmusi, Felix Mnthali, Yukiko Morimoto, Lioba Moshi, Francis Moto, Lupenga Mphande, Angaluki Muaka, Salikoko Mufwene, John Mugane, Stephen Neale, Deo Ngonyani, Armindo Ngunga, Samuel Obeng, Stanley Peters, Daisy Ross, Linda Sarmecanic, Antonia Folarin Schleicher, Russell Schuh, F. E. M. K. Senkoro, Ron Simango, Neil Smith, Nhlanhla Thwala, Paul Tiyambe Zeleza, and Anne Zribi-Hertz.

I remain forever grateful to the students and colleagues that I have had the pleasure to work with at the University of Malawi, San José State University, and at the University of California, Berkeley. They have contributed more to this work than is suggested by the lack of mention of specific names.

Invitations from institutions in England, France, Germany, Hong Kong, Malawi, Mexico, Norway, South Africa, and Swaziland contributed tremendously to the articulation of my views about Bantu linguistic structure. I thank them all. Writing of the manuscript was facilitated by invitations to teach courses on Bantu morphosyntax and linguistic theory at La Universidad de Sonora in Hermosillo, Mexico (2001), at the University of Hong Kong (2002), and at the School of Oriental and African Studies, University of London (2003). I am grateful to Gabriela Caballero de Hernández for making available her notes of the course in Sonora. Thanks to David Boyk and John Wuorenmaa for assistance with technical details of formatting and proof-reading.

Travel has also meant dependence on friends for support and much else. For paying attention to my personal comfort and entertainment, I am very grateful to Sheila Mmusi, C. Themba Msimang, Sizwe Satyo, Moloko Sepota, Sello Sithole, and Nhlanhla Thwala in South Africa; to Euphrasia Kwetemba in Paris, France; to Adriana Barreras, Isabel Barreras, Zarina Estrada Fernández, in Hermosillo, Mexico, and to Maria Eugénia Vazquez Laslop, and Victor Manuel Hernández, in Mexico City; and to Adams Bodomo in Hong Kong. Thanks to the staff of Hotel La Finca in Hermosillo, Mexico, and of the Island Pacific Hotel in Hong Kong, for hospitality and for providing a nice working environment.

I am very fortunate to have David Mason, Francis Mseka, Deedah Steels, and Mick Steels as friends in the United Kingdom. These, together with Bernard Harte, Willis Kabambe, John Kandulu, Jack Mapanje, and Henry Matiti, have always ensured that my trips to England are memorable. Thanks guys.

My visits to, and work in, Malawi would have been far less enjoyable were it not for the hospitality offered by my friends there. For always keeping a place for me and showing me that they are glad I came, I thank Pascal Kishindo, Wisdom Mchungula, Tony Mita, Al Mtenje, Aubrey Nankhuni, Southwood Ng'oma, George Nnensa, Fred Phiri, Khumbo Phiri, Sandra Phiri, Garbett Thyangathyanga, and Ellen Giessler Tiyesi.

I thank my children for showing me the world and increasing my love of, and respect for, the peoples in it, through being scattered all over it, from the far east (Japan), through Africa and Europe, to the far west (California). To Sam, Sarah, David, Chipo, Linda, Kapanga, and Yamikani, thanks for the efforts to keep me young and focused.

To my aunts Mrs. F. Malani, Mrs. K. Mapondo, Mrs. Lillian Bai and her husband Mr. Joseph Bai, and to my uncle Mr. William Ndembo, I remain grateful for their enduring love and support.

I am grateful to Martin James Elmer, Marty Goodman, Iris Grace, Paul Guillory, Tim and Galen Hill, Judith Khaya, P. J. MacAlpine, Tiyanjana Maluwa, Alex Mkandawire, Gerald Mosley, Mohamed Muqtar, Isaiah Nengo, Frazier Nyasulu, Max Reid, Dick Santoro, and other friends already mentioned, for being extremely supportive when times were bleak. I thank my pastor, Reverend John H. Green, at St. Luke Missionary Baptist Church in Richmond, California, for spiritual guidance.

I am very grateful to the staff of Cambridge University Press, especially to Helen Barton, Kay McKechnie, Lucille Murby, and Andrew Winnard, for their help, and for careful editing of the final text.

Finally, the soccer community in the East Bay of the San Francisco Bay Area has provided much-needed diversion from academic pursuits. I thank the Clubs in the Golden State Soccer League of the California Youth Soccer Association, especially San Pablo United Youth Soccer Club, for showing me the joys of a soccer referee. In Malawi, the teams participating in Mtaya Football League in Nkhotakota, and SM Galaxy Football Team in Ndirande, have contributed greatly to making my visits there absolutely wonderful. To all I say zíkomo kwámbíli, asanteni sana, yewo chomene, muchas gracias.

Abbreviations

appl	applicative suffix
asp	aspectual
assoc	associative marker
caus	causative suffix
clt	clitic
cond	conditional
cont	continuous
cop	copula
dem	demonstrative
dim	diminutive
dir	directional marker
distdem	distal demonstrative
fut	future-tense marker
fv	final vowel
hab	habitual
impl	imploring
inf	infinitive marker
loc	locative marker
mod	modal
neg-cop	negative copula
nom	nominal
NP	noun phrase
OM	object marker
perf	perfective marker
pass	passive
pl	plural marker
poss	possessive
pref	prefix
pres	present-tense marker
prog	progressive
proxdem	proximal demonstrative

pst	past-tense marker
Q	question word
recip	reciprocal morpheme (affix)
reflex	reflexive morpheme
rel	relative marker
relpro	relative pronoun
SM	subject marker
stat	stative
subjun	subjunctive
VP	verb phrase
VR	verb root
VS	verb stem

Tone marking

High tone, as in *á*.
Falling tone, as in *û*.
Rising tone, as in *ě*.
Low tones are unmarked.

1

Introduction

1.1   General remarks

Chichewa is a language of the Bantu language group in the Benue-Congo branch of the Niger-Kordofania language family. It is spoken in parts of east, central and southern Africa. Since 1968 it has been the dominant language in the east African nation of Malawi where, until recently, it also served as that country's national language. It is spoken in Mozambique (especially in the provinces of Tete and Niassa), in Zambia (especially in the Eastern Province), as well as in Zimbabwe where, according to some estimates, it ranks as the third most widely used local language, after Shona and Ndebele. The countries of Malawi, Zambia, and Mozambique constitute, by far, the central location of Chichewa. Because of the national language policy adopted by the Malawi government, which promoted Chichewa through active educational programs, media usage, and other research activities carried out under the auspices of the Chichewa Board, out of a population of around 9 million, upwards of 65 percent have functional literacy or active command of this language. In Mozambique, the language goes by the name of Chinyanja, and it is native to 3.3 percent of a population numbering approximately 11.5 million. In Tete province it is spoken by 41.7 percent of a population of 777,426 and it is the first language of 7.2 percent of the population of Niassa province, whose population totals 506,974 (see Firmino 1995). In Zambia with a population of 9.1 million, Chinyanja is the first language of 16 percent of the population and is used and/or understood by at least 42 percent of the population, according to a survey conducted in 1978 (cf. Kashoki 1978). It is one of the main languages of Zambia, ranking second after Chibemba. In fact, out of the 9.1 million people of that country, it is estimated that 36 percent are Bemba, 18 percent Nyanja, 15 percent Tonga, 8 percent Barotze, with the remainder consisting of the other ethnic groups including the Mombwe, Tumbuka, and the Northwestern peoples (see Kalipeni 1998). The figures show that at least upwards of 6 million people have fluent command of Chichewa/Chinyanja.

As indicated, the language is identified by the label Chinyanja in all the countries mentioned above except, until recently, in Malawi. It is commonplace to see many

1

publications or former school examinations making reference to the language as Chinyanja/Chichewa. The factors that led to such a multiplicity of labels will not be spelt out here. The relevant details are readily available elsewhere (see Mchombo website, http://www.humnet.ucla.edu/humnet/aflang/chichewa/).

1.2   General features of Chichewa

In its structural organization, Chichewa adheres very closely to the general patterns of Bantu languages. Its nominal system comprises a number of gender classes characteristic of Bantu in general. The noun classes play a significant role in the agreement patterning of the language. Thus, modifiers of nouns agree with the head noun in the relevant features of gender and number, as will be illustrated below (see section 1.3 below). In its verbal structure, Chichewa is typical of Bantu languages in displaying an elaborate agglutinative structure. The verb comprises a verb root or radical, to which suffixes or extensions are added (cf. Guthrie 1962) to form the verb stem. The extensions affect the number of expressible nominal arguments that the stem can support. In other words, verbal extensions affect the argument structure of the verb (Dembetembe 1987; Dlayedwa 2002; Guthrie 1962; Hoffman 1991; Mchombo 1999a, 2001, 2002a, b; Satyo 1985). To the verb stem are added proclitics which encode syntactically oriented information. This includes the expression of Negation, Tense/Aspect, Subject and Object markers, Modals, Conditional markers, Directional markers, etc. The structural organization of the verb will be discussed in detail below. Motivation for the suggested structural organization will be provided.

With regard to phonological aspects, Chichewa is a tone language, displaying features of lexical and grammatical tone. Basically, Chichewa has two level tones, high (H), and low (L). Contour tones also occur but then only as a combination of these level tones, usually on long syllables (Mtenje 1986b). In its segmental phonology, Chichewa has the basic organization of five vowel phonemes. The verbal unit manifests aspects of vowel harmony. This will be illustrated in sections that focus on the structure of the verb. In its syllable structure, Chichewa has the basic CV structure common in Bantu (Mtenje 1980). These issues will be taken up in the next chapter. At this juncture, attention will be turned to the noun classification system and related issues.

1.3   The classification of nouns

A major feature of Bantu languages is the classification of nouns into various classes; another is the elaborate agglutinative nature of the verbal structure.

The latter will be reviewed in detail in subsequent chapters. With regard to nominal morphology, Chichewa displays the paradigmatic case of nouns maintaining, at the minimum, a bimorphemic structure. This consists in the nouns having a nominal stem and a nominal prefix. The prefix encodes grammatically relevant information of gender (natural) and number. This plays a role in agreement between the nouns and other grammatical classes in construction with them.

Let us look at the system of noun classification in Bantu languages. Typical examples of nouns are provided by the following:

(1)   chi-soti 'hat'   zi-soti 'hats'
        m-kóndo 'spear' mi-kóndo 'spears'

Of interest is the question of the basis for this classification of nouns. This is an issue that still awaits a definitive response. The formal structure of the noun, which does have some bearing on its class membership, has relevance to the regulation of the agreement patterns of the languages. In brief, noun modifiers are marked for agreement with the class features of the head noun, and these features are also what are reflected in the SM and the OM in the verbal morphology. This can be illustrated by the following:

(2) a.   Chi-soti ch-ángá ch-á-tsópanó   chi-ja   chí-ma-sangaláts-á a-lenje.
         7-hat   7SM-my 7SM-assoc-now 7SM-that 7SM-hab-please-fv 2-hunters
         'That new hat of mine pleases hunters.'

   b.   M-kóndó w-angá   w-á-tsópanó   u-ja   ú-ma-sangaláts-á   alenje.
         3-spear 3SM-my 3SM-assoc-now 3SM-that 3SM-hab-please-fv 2-hunters
         'That new spear of mine pleases hunters.'

In these sentences, the words in construction with the nouns are marked for agreement with that head noun (the actual agreement markers in these examples are *chi* and *u*; the *i* vowel in *chi* is elided when followed by a vowel, and the *u* is replaced by the glide *w* in a similar environment). Chichewa is a head-initial language; hence, the head noun precedes its modifiers within a noun phrase. The formal patterns that yield the singular and the plural forms are, traditionally, identified by a particular numbering system now virtually standard in Bantu linguistics (Bleek 1862/69; Watters 1989). Consider the following data:

(3) a.   m-nyamăta 'boy'   a-nyamăta 'boys'
         m-lenje 'hunter'   a-lenje 'hunters'
         m-kázi 'woman'   a-kázi 'women'

   b.   m-kóndo 'spear'   mi-kóndo 'spears'
         mŭ-nda 'garden'   mĭ-nda 'gardens'
         m-kángo 'lion'   mi-kángo 'lions'

    c.   tsamba 'leaf'   ma-samba 'leaves'
         duwa 'flower'   ma-luwa 'flowers'
         phanga 'cave'   ma-panga 'caves'

    d.   chi-sa 'nest'   zi-sa 'nests'
         chi-tŏsi 'chicken dropping' zi-tŏsi 'chicken droppings'
         chi-pútu 'grass stubble'   zi-pútu 'grass stubble'

These classes show part of the range of noun classification that is characteristic of Bantu languages. The full range of noun classes for Chichewa is presented in table 1.1 below; the class numbers used in the examples reflect the classes listed in that table. The singular forms of the first group above constitute class 1, and its plural counterpart is class 2. These classes tend to be dominated by nouns that denote animate things although not all animate things are in this class. In fact, it also includes some inanimate objects. The next singular class is class 3, and its plural version is class 4. This runs on to classes 5, 6, 7, and 8. There is also class 1a. This class consists of nouns whose agreement patterns are those of class 1 but whose nouns lack the *m(u)* prefix found in the class 1 nouns. The plural of such nouns is indicated by prefixing *a* to the word. For instance, the noun *kalúlu* 'hare' whose plural is *akalúlu* typifies this class. Each of these classes has a specific class marker and a specific agreement marker. Beginning with class 2, the agreement markers are, respectively, *a, u, i, li, a, chi, zi.* Class 1 is marked by *mu* (or syllabic *m*), *u*, and *a*, depending on the category of the modifier.

Consider the following:

(4)   M-lenje m-módzi a-na-bwél-á   ndí mí-kóndo.
        1-hunter 1SM-one 1SM-pst-come-fv with 4-spears
        'One hunter came with spears.'

In this, the numeral *módzi* 'one' is marked with the agreement marker *m* but the verb has *a* for the subject marker. The *u* is used with demonstratives and when the segment that follows is a vowel. This seems to apply to most cases, regardless of whether the vowel in question is a tense/aspect marker, associative marker or part of a stem, such as with possessives. The possessives could themselves be analyzed as comprising a possessive stem to which an associative marker is prefixed (cf. Thwala 1995). Consider the following.

(5)   M-lenje w-ánú   u-ja   w-á   nthábwala w-a-thyol-a
        1-hunter 1SM-your 1SM-that SM-assoc 10-humor 1SM-perf-break-fv
        mi-kóndo.
        4-spears
        'That humorous hunter of yours has broken the spears.'

In this sentence, the *w* is the glide that replaces *u* when a vowel follows, regardless of the function associated with that vowel.

Although most of the nouns are bimorphemic, there are a number of cases where a further prefix, which may mark either diminution or augmentation, is added to an already prefixed noun. This is shown in the following:

(6)   Ka-m-lenje k-ánú   ka-ja   k-á   nthábwala k-a-thyol-a
        12-1-hunter 12SM-your 12SM-that 12-assoc 10-humor 12SM-perf-break-fv
        ti-mi-kóndo.
        13-4-spears
        'That small humorous hunter of yours has broken the tiny spears.'

In this sentence, the pre-prefixes *ka* for singular and *ti* for plural, are added to nouns to convey the sense of diminutive size. These pre-prefixes then control the agreement patterns (cf. Bresnan and Mchombo 1995), which provides the rationale for regarding them as governing separate noun classes. In fact, in other Bantu languages, for instance Xhosa and Zulu, the nouns have a pre-prefix that is attached to the "basic" prefix (cf. Dlayedwa 2002; Satyo 1985; van der Spuy 1989). In Xhosa, for instance, nouns consist of a pre-prefix, basic prefix, and a noun stem. The pre-prefix and basic prefix are involved in the agreement patterns. One significant point to be made is that locatives also control agreement patterns. Consider the following:

(7)   Ku   mudzi   kw-ánu   kú-ma-sangaláts-á alĕndo.
        17-at 3-village 17SM-your 17-hab-please-fv   2-visitors
        'Your village (i.e. the location) pleases visitors.'

This gives such locatives the appearance of being class markers. It has been argued that locatives in Chichewa are not really prepositions that mark grammatical case but, rather, class markers (for some discussion, see Bresnan 1991, 1995).

At this stage it would be useful to provide the full range of noun classes for Chichewa. This is presented in table 1.1. Note that some classes are not present in this language. For instance, Chichewa lacks class 11, with prefix reconstructed as *du* in proto-Bantu.

Some of the classes have prefixes which are starred. These classes consist of nouns which, normally, lack the indicated prefix in the noun morphology. Samples of class 5 nouns are provided above. Most of the nouns in classes 9 and 10 begin with a nasal but there are no overt changes in their morphological composition that correlate with number. The number distinction is reflected in the agreement markers rather than in the overt form of the noun. Examples of class 9/10 nouns are: *nyŭmba* 'house(s),' *nthenga* 'feather(s),' *mphîni* 'tattoo(s),' *nkhôndo* 'war.' Class 15 consists of infinitive verbs. The infinitive marker *ku-* regulates the agreement patterns, just like the diminutives (classes 12 and 13) and locatives. The infinitives are thus regarded as constituting a separate class although, just as is the case with the locatives, with minor exceptions, there are no nouns that are peculiar to this

Table 1.1 *Noun classes in Chichewa*

Class		Prefix		Subj marker		Obj marker	
SG	PL	SG	PL	SG	PL	SG	PL
1	2	m(u)-	a-	a-	a-	m(u)	wa
3	4	m(u)-	mi-	u-	i-	u	i
5	6	*li-	ma-	li-	a-	li	wa
7	8	chi-	zi-	chi-	zi-	chi	zi
9	10	*N-	*N-	i-	zi-	i	zi
12	13	ka-	ti-	ka-	ti-	ka	ti
14	6	u-	ma-	u	a	u	wa
15		ku-	ku	ku			
16		pa-	pa	pa			
17		ku-	ku	ku			
18		m(u)-	m(u)	m(u)			

class. The minor exceptions to locatives have to do with the words *pansi* 'down,' *kunsi* 'underneath,' *panja* 'outside of a place,' *kunja* '(the general) outside,' *pano* 'here (at this spot),' *kuno* 'here (hereabouts),' *muno* 'in here.' With these, the locative prefixes *pa, ku,* and *mu* are attached to the stems *-nsi, -nja,* and *-no,* which are bound. The agreement pattern regulated by the infinitive marker *ku-* is exemplified by the following:

(8)　　Ku-ímbá　　kw-anú　　　kú-ma-sangaláts-á　　alenje.
　　　　15inf-sing　15SM-your　15SM-hab-please-fv　2-hunters
　　　　'Your singing pleases hunters.'

1.4　　On the status of prefixes

At a more general level of analysis the question arises with respect to the status of the nominal prefixes. Are they morphological units that combine with the stem in the morphological component of grammar, or are they syntactic elements that form a phonological word with the stem? In an analysis of Shona, a Bantu language spoken in Zimbabwe, Myers (1991) argues that the prefixes in nominal structure are syntactic determiners which form a phonological word with the stem. The structure of the noun could be represented as below, for constructions with the diminutive or the locative.

(9)　　N+possessive:
　　　　*mpando u-ánga　*ka(mpando) wánga　kampando ka-ánga*
　　　　chair　 my　　 dim-chair　 my　　'my little chair'

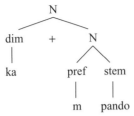

Figure 1.1

In this the prefixes comprise syntactic determiners that combine with the stem at the level of phonology. There is thus no morphological component dedicated to word formation. In fact, in other analyses, mainly couched within the Principles and Parameters Theory, information pertaining to number and gender is factored into separate structural projections, with movement accounting for their subsequent realization within the same overt form (cf. Carstens 1991). These analyses have been countered in the work of Bresnan and Mchombo (1995) on the basis of lexical integrity. Specifically, Bresnan and Mchombo noted that:

> morphological constituents of words are lexical and sublexical categories – stems and affixes – while the syntactic constituents of phrases have words as the minimal, unanalyzable units; and syntactic ordering principles do not apply to morphemic structures. As a result, morphemic order is fixed, even when syntactic word order is free; the directionality of "headedness" of sublexical structures may differ from supralexical structures; and the internal structure of words is opaque to certain syntactic processes.   (Bresnan and Mchombo 1995: 1)

Adopting the general strategy that the internal structure of words is opaque to syntactic processes, Bresnan and Mchombo adduce evidence which demonstrates that such syntactic processes as extraction, conjoinability, gapping, inbound anaphora, and phrasal recursivity do not apply to Bantu nouns. This undermines the syntactic analysis of the nominal structure in Bantu proposed by Myers as well as Carstens, and maintains a morphological structure of the nouns. The one area where a syntactic analysis appears plausible is in locative nouns. In these, the agreement patterns appeared to alternate between agreement with the locative or with the class of the basic noun. Such alternative concord is impossible with the diminutives, where only the outer prefix controls agreement. With locatives, on the other hand, the agreement can, sometimes, be with the inner class marker. Consider the following:

(10) a.   pa mpando pa-ánga (loc)
         on the chair my

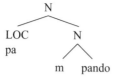

Figure 1.2

However, this also allows for the following expression with the possessive agreeing with the basic class marker of *mpando* 'chair':

b.   pampando wánga

Such alternation in the concord seems to indicate that the locative must have a syntactic structure since the opacity of the word to syntactic processes is violated. In the analysis provided by Bresnan and Mchombo the claim was that the locative marker may have indeed originated as a syntactic element but that it has undergone steady morphologization. The alternative concord appears to indicate that the morphologization process is not complete. In brief, the nouns in Bantu satisfy the tests for lexical integrity, indicating their status as morphological words. The noun class markers are not syntactic determiners but morphological units, specifically, prefixes, combining morphologically with the stem to yield the noun.

2

Phonetics and phonology

2.1   The consonant system

In its consonantal inventory, Chichewa has a range of sounds. These include plosives, nasals, fricatives, affricates, glides, and an alveolar lateral. Although in standard orthography it is claimed that the trill [r] is present, in allophonic variation with the lateral [l], it is a sound that is not common in speech. The rule concerning the distribution of [r] is that it appears after the front vowel phonemes [i] and [e], as in Luganda, a language spoken in Uganda (Katamba 1984). However, the rule is not general. In its formulation in the Chichewa Orthography Rules, it is immediately accompanied by the rider that the rule does not apply when the conditioning environment is created by affixation. Thus, according to the rule, [r] should occur in the following words, as indicated:

(1)   mbendéra 'flag'
         mchíra   'tail'
         mpira   'ball'
         -kwera   'climb, ride'
         -bwera   'come (back)'
         -piríra   'endure, persevere'
         -kolera   'burn, blaze (of fire)'

However, [l] should not be changed to [r] when the conditioning environment results from affixation. For instance, one of the forms of the copula 'be' is the irregular verb *-li*. Consider the following expressions:

(2) a.   Mu-li   bwánji?
         You (pl)-be how?
         'How are you?'

    b.   A-li   bwino.
         3rd sing-be well
         'S/he is fine.'

The first-person-singular pronominal marker in Chichewa is *ndi,* and the first-person-plural marker is *ti.* If either one of these is attached to the copula *-li,* the lateral [l] would be in the environment for the trill, as shown below:

(3) a.   Ndi-li   bwino.
          1st sing-be well
          'I am well.'

   b.   Ti-li   bwino.
          1st pl-be well
          'We are well.'

According to the rule, the lateral of the copula should be a trill. However, the lateral does not become a trill and even the rules for Chichewa orthography clearly prohibit the change of the lateral to a trill in such environments (Chichewa Board 1990). The reality is that even in the cases where the trill is supposed to be legitimate, in ordinary pronunciation of the words given above, it is the lateral that is used, not the trill. In recent revisions of the orthography of the language, it has been proposed to drop the trill altogether.[1] This move constitutes a major effort to reflect the patterns of speech of the people.[2]

Another significant feature of the sound system of Chichewa is aspiration. Plosives and affricates have aspirated counterparts and aspiration, like voicing, is phonemic in the language. The following minimal pairs may help illustrate the point:

(4)   -pala 'scrape'   phala 'porridge'
         -kola 'entangle, catch in a trap' -khola 'fit well'
         -kula 'grow'   -khula 'rub'

The consonantal system is represented in table 2.1

In ordinary orthography, the following conventions are adopted:

[ɲ] = ny   Chinyanja 'Nyanja language'
[ŋ] = ng' ng'ombe   'cow'
[ŋg] = ng ngongŏle   'debt'
[tʃ] = ch chikoti   'whip'
[dʒ] = j   jando   'circumcision ceremony'
[ʒ] = zy   zyolika   'be upside down (as a bat)'[3]

[1] The director of the Centre for Language Studies, University of Malawi, Al Mtenje, in personal communication, indicated that doing so would help the orthography better reflect speech. Further, this is part of a trend toward standardization of orthography among languages of southern Africa, initiated by the Linguistic Association of SADC Universities (LASU).

[2] Because of the orthographic convention that prevailed in print for a long time, most newsreaders, in trying to remain faithful to the written form, pronounced the trill in the words written with it. There is, therefore, a touch of irony in the disappearance of [r] from the orthography at a time when there may have been something of a resurgence of the sound among some speakers.

[3] The voiced palatal fricative is rare in Chichewa. It is attested in certain varieties of Chinyanja, for instance, the variety spoken in north-west Mozambique, in the Niassa province.

Table 2.1 *Consonants*

	Bilabial	Labio-dental	Alveolar	Palatal	Velar
Plosives	p^h		t^h		k^h
	p b		t d		k g
Nasals	m		n	ɲ	ŋ
Fricatives		f v	s z	ʃ ʒ	
Affricates			ts dz	tʃ dʒ	
Laterals			l		
Trill			r		
Semi-consonants	w			y	

There is a series of prenasalized stops that, in the orthography, are simply written as a sequence of the nasal and the stop, aspirated in the case of voiceless stops and affricates. The following provide illustration: [$^m p^h$] as in *mphánda* 'tree branch,' [$^n t^h$] as in *nthenga* 'feather(s),' [$^N k^h$] as in *ŋkhono* 'snail(s),' [$^m b$] as in *mbólo* 'penis,' [$^n d$] as in *ndeu* 'a fight,' and [$^ŋ g$] as in *ŋgoŋgŏle* 'debt.' Also, involving affricates, there is [$^n tʃ^h$], as in *nchénche* 'fly/flies' and [$^n dʒ$] as in *njóka* 'snake(s).' All nouns beginning with such clusters are included in classes 9/10 in Chichewa. The voiceless palatal affricate [tʃ] is ordinarily indicated by the letters *ch*. Naturally, this posed problems for the indication of aspiration, since [h] is normally used to signal aspiration. The decision to use *ch* for the affricate was an innovation in Chichewa. Previously, the affricate was indicated by the letter *c* alone. Older publications have the word *chinyanja* spelt as *Ci-nyanja*, with the letter *h* used solely for aspiration. The shift to the use of *ch* for the affricate was decreed by the then Life President of the Republic of Malawi, the late Dr. Hastings Kamuzu Banda, influenced by the English language. The problem then arose as to how to indicate aspiration in the case of an affricate and it was decided to use the letter *t*. Thus the following minimal pair shows the use of *t* as a marker of aspiration:

(5)   kŭ-cha 'to dawn' kŭ-tcha 'to set a trap'

Again, recent efforts to revise and standardize the orthographies of the languages of east, central, and southern Africa have led to the decision to revert to the old system. The affricate is to be indicated by the single letter *c*; the letter *h* is to be used for words that involve it or for marking aspiration.[4]

---

[4] According to the director of the Centre for Language Studies at the University of Malawi, although LASU will make broad recommendations regarding orthography, individual language associations may still be left to decide whether to adopt specific recommendations; for instance, the recommendation to use [h] for aspiration may be relaxed in the orthographic representation of the affricate [tS] as *c* rather than *ch* because of the already-established use of *ch* to represent the unaspirated affricate.

It should also be pointed out that older publications reflect the labio-dental frica-tives [f] and [v] as affricates. They were transcribed as [pf] and [bv] respectively. It was noted by the Chichewa Board that in the speech of the people of Malawi, there was no longer affrication in words involving those sounds. Thus, words such as *fúpa* 'bone' and *mafúpa* 'bones,' or *vuzi* '(single) pubic hair' and *mavuzi* 'pubic hair,' do not have affricates any more. Older orthographic forms of these would have them written down as *pfúpa, mapfúpa, bvuzi,* and *mabvuzi.* This convention is, apparently, still used in the Chinyanja spoken in Zambia (cf. Lehmann 2002). It is certainly not the case in the variety of Chichewa that is described here, which represents the dialect spoken in central and southern parts of Malawi. The variety that was described by Mark Hanna Watkins (1937) may have had those sounds, but it was an older version of Chichewa, and, further, it was the variety then spoken in the northern part of central Malawi, bordering with Chitumbuka, which is spoken in the northern region of the country. The language change of losing affrication in these sounds, and reducing them to fricatives, appears to have affected that variety as well.

2.2   The vowel system

Chichewa has the simple five-vowel system indicated in figure 2.1.

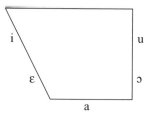

Figure 2.1

The vowels can be divided into those that are [+mid] and those that are [−mid]. This distinction plays a role in the patterns of vowel harmony that occur in the verb stem (Katamba 1984; Mchombo 1998; Mtenje 1985). The general pattern is that mid vowels co-occur and the non-mid vowels co-occur. This is only violated in a few instances, usually when the reciprocal suffix is added. The reciprocal is realized by the morpheme *-an-*. It does not have variants. Consequently, it gets suffixed to any verb stem that gets a reciprocal reading. It does, nonetheless, influence the shape of the affixes that may get affixed after it. This will be discussed further in sections on argument structure.

2.3   Syllable structure

The syllable structure for Chichewa is the canonical CV (Mtenje 1980). Consonant clusters are permitted, but subject to some phonotactic constraints. While any consonant can appear in the C position, in CCV structures the first C cannnot be any one of the glides. In fact, the palatal glide appears to be more restricted than the labial glide. For instance, there are words such as the following: *phwanya* 'smash,' *khwacha* 'erase, cancel,' *bwánji* 'how,' *dwala* 'fall ill,' *kwilila* 'bury,' *gwaza* 'stab,' *mwalíla* 'die,' *thyola* 'break,' *pyola* 'go past, overshoot, overtake.' The claim has been made that when glides appear, they are the result of phonological processes that disrupt vowel sequences. In fact, in a detailed study of the derivational phonology of Chichewa and aspects of its syllable structure constraints, Mtenje (1980) argued that various phonological rules had functional unity or a conspiracy effect. They disrupt VV sequences to restore the canonical CV syllable organization. These include rules of deletion, epenthesis, glide formation, etc. In Chichewa the [w] glide appears to arise in environments where the vowel [u] precedes some other vowel, which probably constitutes a separate syllable. The glide [y] normally involves the presence of the vowel [i] before another vowel, and, usually, is not preceded by a consonant. This is evident in morpheme concatenation. Consider the following:

(6) a.   Mkángó u-á >wá   mfúmu
    3-lion 3SM-assoc 9-chief
    'The lion of the chief'

  b.   Mikángó i-á>yá   mfúmu
    4-lions 4SM-assoc 9-chief
    'The lions of the chief'

On the other hand, note the following:

  c.   Mkángó sí-ú-ku-fúná   nyâma.
    3-lion neg-3SM-pres-want 9-meat
    'The lion does not want meat.'

The normal pronunciation of *síúkufúná* is *súkufúná* 'it does not want.' In this the vowel [i] is simply elided instead of forming a glide.

When the syllable consists of more than two consonants, the initial one is a nasal. This is exemplified by such words as *mphwáyi* 'procrastination,' *nkhwángwa* 'axe.'

2.4   Syllable structure and morpheme structure

In general, words observe the phonotactic constraints of the language. Morphemes, on the other hand, can depart in their syllabic organization from the general pattern of the language. In Chichewa, and in Bantu languages in general, there is non-isomorphism between the morphological organization of the verb stem and the syllable structure requirements. The verb root or radical is normally bound, ending in a consonant. Take the verb for 'cook,' *phik-a*. Here the verb root is *phik-* and the vowel *-a* at the end is a separate morpheme. It is normally referred to simply as the final vowel (fv). It is, effectively, the vowel that helps avoidance of violations of syllable structure constraints. The verb extensions, such as the applicative, causative, stative, reciprocal, etc., all have a -VC- organization. The verb which means 'to have things cooked for each other' has the following morphological structure:

(7)   phik-its-il-an-a
         cook-caus-appl-recip-fv
         'cause to cook for each other'

The extensions all have -VC- organization. When the final vowel is added then there is resyllabification, which restores conformity to the phonotactics of the language. In this respect, the verbal extensions differ from the proclitics that are prefixed to the verb stem. Those have the canonical syllable organization of CV. This difference will comprise one aspect of the motivation for a specific conception of the structure of the verbal unit in Chichewa. Note that the verb stem, which displays this non-isomorphism between morphological structure and syllable structure, is also the domain in which vowel harmony operates in Chichewa and some of the other Bantu languages. Vowel harmony spreads to the extensions from the root but it does not apply in the domain of the pre-verb-stem proclitics.

2.5   Stress assignment

Associated with syllable structure are such prosodic features as stress and tone. Chichewa manifests the feature of fixed stress that is common in Bantu languages. Within a phonological word primary stress is normally assigned to the penultimate syllable. In a word with the syllable structure shown in figure 2.2 below, stress would be assigned to the syllable indicated in bold.

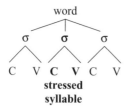

Figure 2.2

The fixedness of stress is demonstrated by stress shift under affixation. Take Swahili, for instance. In Swahili *andika* means 'write' and the stress is on the penult *ndi*. When the verb extensions such as the causative, applicative, and reciprocal are affixed, the stress shifts to the penult. This is illustrated in the following:

(8) andíka   write
     andik-ísh-a   write-caus-fv   'cause to write'
     andik-í-a   write-appl-fv   'write for/to'
     andik-ish-i-án-a write-caus-appl-recip-fv 'cause to write for each other'

Given that the verbal unit arguably comprises a verb stem, and is separate from the material prefixed to it, it is an interesting question as to whether there is an internal boundary, demarcating the verb stem from the proclitics, and whether the two comprise domains for wordhood. The relevance of stress assignment would be that if there were more than one primary stress within the verbal unit, then there would be grounds for recognizing a phonological word boundary within the verbal unit. So far, evidence based on stress assignment does not support the possibility of such compound word formation. Another prosodic feature that is normally borne by syllables is tone. It has been indicated above that Chichewa is a tone language, manifesting lexical and grammatical tone. A few remarks about tone in Chichewa are in order.

2.6   Tone

Chichewa has two level tones: low (L) and (H). Contour tones arise from combinations of these level tones. Among the nouns, tonal contrasts mark difference between words which are identical in their segmental composition. Consider the following:

(9) m.té.ngo 'tree (3)'   kh.ûngu 'blindness (5)'
     m.te.ngo 'price (3)' kh.ŭngu 'skin'

Within the verbal unit the interest has been in the behavior of tone within both the verb stem, i.e. the verb root and its extensions or suffixes, and the proclitics. As first noted by Mtenje (1986b), the verb roots can be grouped into those that are high-toned and those that are toneless, with the low tone as the default. Verbal extensions, which include the affixes for the causative, applicative, reciprocal, stative or neuter, passive, appear to be basically toneless. However, they inherit the tone of the root to which they are suffixed. Consider the following:

(10) -imba   sing
     -i.mb.its.a   sing-caus-   'cause to sing'
     imb.its.il.a   sing-caus-appl   'cause to sing for'
     imb-its-an-a   sing-caus-recip   'make each other sing'

The verb *-imba* 'sing' is low-toned. When the causative morpheme *-its-* is attached, to derive the verb stem meaning 'cause to sing,' the affix is itself low-toned. When the applicative morpheme *-il-* is added to that, yielding the verb stem 'cause to sing for,' it is also low-toned. The same holds for the reciprocalized causative. When these morphemes are added to a high-toned verb, such as *péza* 'find,' they become high-toned:

(11)	-péza	find	
	-pézétsa	find-caus	'cause to find'
	-pézéla	find-appl	'find for'
	-pézána	find-recip	'find each other'
	-pézétsána	find-caus-recip	'cause to find each other'

The claim that verbal extensions are underlyingly toneless but inherit the tone of the root is not true of all the extensions. The passive *-idw-* appears to be high-toned although the situation gets complicated by the fact that it is normally the extension that gets attached last. As such, it also appears in the normal position for stress. That is similarly true of the stative *-ik-*. Still, Mtenje's observation seems to hold by and large. This led him to claim that the verb stem in Chichewa appears to lack the characteristics of a true tone language, displaying instead features of an accentual system (Mtenje 1986a, b).

On the other hand, the proclitics appear to have their own tones and they affect the tonal pattern of the whole verbal unit. For instance, tense markers have tone features that may spread to the verb stem and affect the tone patterning in that domain. For instance, the tense/aspect marker *-ma-* indicates either present habitual or past continuous or habitual. The two readings are tonally distinct, as shown by the sentences below:

(12) a. Njovu   zi-ma-ímb-íts-án-á   mingóli.
         10-elephants 10SM-psthab-play-caus-recip-fv 4-harmonicas
         'The elephants were making each other play harmonicas.'

     b. Njovu   zí-ma-imb-its-án-á   mingóli.
         10-elephants 10SM-hab-play-caus-recip-fv   4-harmonicas
         'The elephants make each other play harmonicas.'

The two examples display different tone patterns of the verb stem. The patterns are induced by the proclitics. This is common in Bantu languages where, when certain grammatical elements (e.g. tense, object, or reflexive markers) are attached to verbs, various tonal alternations occur. A proposal made by Mtenje is that of setting up a tone lexicon which such grammatical elements have access to. They select the tones that characterize them and these can shift or otherwise influence the tonal pattern of the verb stem (Chimombo and Mtenje 1989, 1991; Mtenje 1987).

The importance of tone in Chichewa extends to syntactic configurations. A few observations will be made here, to be taken up in some detail later.

2.7 Relative-clause formation

The relevance of tone to syntactic structure in Chichewa is illustrated here with relative-clause formation. In Chichewa, the relative clause modifies a nominal head that is outside that clause. Ordinarily the relative clause is introduced by *-méne* 'that' to which an agreement marker of the class of the head noun is attached. If the head noun originated as the object of the verb in the relative clause, the verb would have either a null element in the object position, identified with the relativized noun, or an object marker which functions as a resumptive pronoun (cf. Biloa 1990; Ngonyani 1999; Sells 1984). The relative clause in Chichewa, just as in English, could be diagrammatically represented as in figure 2.3.

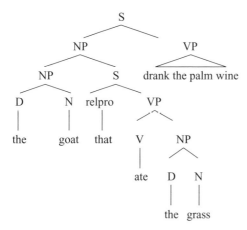

Figure 2.3

Consider the following:

(13)   Alenje   a-ku-sáká   mkángo.
        2-hunters 2SM-pres-hunt 3SM-lion
        'The hunters are hunting a lion.'

From this one gets the following relative construction:

(14) a.   Mkángó u-méné alenje   á-ku-sáka
           3-lion   3SM-rel 2-hunters 2SM-pres-hunt
           'The lion that the hunters are hunting'

What is significant here is the tone on the subject marker of the verb *á-ku-sáka* in the relative clause. The tone pattern appears to be induced by either the presence of the relative marker or the fact that it is a relative construction. Since the tone pattern marks the syntactic configuration as a relative construction, the relative marker can be dropped without changing its status as a relative clause. Take the initial sentence above, and notice how the change on its tonal pattern affects the nature of the syntactic construction. The expression (13) above is a declarative sentence. On the other hand, if the tone is changed, so that it reads as below:

b.   Alenje á-ku-sáká mkángo

the expression is no longer a declarative statement but a relative construction, meaning 'the hunters who are hunting the lion.' In English such deletion of the relative marker would lead to ungrammaticality as the relativized NP would be construed as a sentence, with attendant garden-path effects. Such involvement of tone with syntactic structure has been commented upon in various works (cf. Bresnan and Mchombo 1986, 1987; Kanerva 1990; Mchombo 1978; Mchombo and Moto 1981). In the work of Bresnan and Mchombo, it was further observed that tone marks the Verb Phrase configuration in Chichewa (see Bresnan and Mchombo 1987). Naturally, such involvement of tone in syntax raises the question as to the nature of the relation between syntax and phonology, syntax and morphology, morphology and phonology, and, as will become evident later, between syntax and discourse.

Like vowel harmony and adherence to syllable structure constraints, in Chichewa verbal extensions behave differently from proclitics with regard to tone. Mtenje noted that there is tone spreading within the verb stem, making the verb stem seem to have characteristics of an accentual system rather than a tone language. This will constitute yet another piece of evidence for proposing a specific structural organization of the verbal unit in this language. The proposed structural organization has consequences for the formalization of grammatical theory.

2.8   Conclusion

In this chapter aspects of the phonological system of Chichewa have been reviewed. We have paid attention to consonantal and vowel systems, to syllable structure, stress and tone patterns, and their implications for the articulation of grammatical theory. In the next chapter, attention will shift to clause structure and verbal morphology, the latter to be pursued in greater detail in discussion of argument structure. The relevance of tone to syntactic structure will receive commentary where appropriate.

3

Clause structure

3.1　Basic word order

The general conception about clause structure in Bantu is that the languages have an SVOX order (cf. Watters 1989). Chichewa fits into this word-order typology. In a simple transitive sentence, the grammatical object follows the verb. This can be shown in sentence (1) below:

(1)　　Mikángo i-ku-sák-á　　　　zigawénga.
　　　　4-lions　4SM-pres-hunt-fv 8-terrorists
　　　　'The lions are hunting the terrorists.'

The object nominal must occur after and be adjacent to the verb. The subject nominal, on the other hand, need not appear before the verb. The subject marker (SM) which appears in the verbal morphology, and duplicates the φ-features of the subject, effectively preserves that nominal's association with the grammatical function of Subject. Thus, the nominal itself could be displaced to postverbal position, as in (2):

(2)　　I-ku-sák-á　　　　zigawénga mikángo.
　　　　4SM-pres-hunt-fv 8-terrorists 4-lions
　　　　'The lions are hunting the terrorists.'

Although the subject nominal can be displaced to appear postverbally, it cannot disrupt the verb–object sequence. Thus sentence (3), below, is ungrammatical:

(3)　　*I-ku-sák-á　　　　mikángo zigawénga
　　　　4SM-pres-hunt-fv 4-lions　8-terrorists

The basic word order is altered when the object marker (OM) is included in the verbal morphology. The OM duplicates the φ-features of the nominal functioning as the object. When it occurs, the OM is attached immediately preceding the verb stem. This is illustrated in sentence (4):

(4)　　Mikángo i-ku-zí-săk-a　　　　zigawénga.
　　　　4-lions　4SM-pres-8OM-hunt-fv 8-terrorists
　　　　'The lions are hunting them, the terrorists.'

With the inclusion of the OM, the nominal arguments can be freely ordered with respect to each other and with respect to the verbal unit. They can also be dropped without inducing ungrammaticality. All of the sentences in (5) below are grammatical and have the same cognitive meaning.

(5) a. Mikángo i-ku-zí-săk-a zigawénga.
   b. I-ku-zí-săk-a mikángo zigawénga.
   c. I-ku-zí-săk-a zigawénga mikángo.
   d. Zigawénga i-ku-zí-săk-a mikángo.
   e. Mikángo zigawénga i-ku-zí-săk-a.
   f. Zigawénga mikángo i-ku-zí-săk-a.
   g. I-ku-zí-săk-a.
      'The lions are hunting the terrorists.'

Sentence (5g), in which there are no overt nominals, has the reading 'they are hunting them.'

Naturally, the observation that the nominal arguments can be omitted in the presence of the SM and OM has raised questions about the nature of the relation between them and the nominal arguments in grammatical structure. In recent studies a wealth of evidence has been amassed to show that the SM and OM are best analyzed as pronominal arguments that are incorporated in the verbal morphology. The nominal arguments are TOPIC elements, licensed by discourse factors (cf. Bresnan and Mchombo 1986, 1987; Demuth and Johnson 1989; Omar 1990; Rubanza 1988). We will examine some of the evidence for this analysis.

3.2   On pronominal incorporation

The evidence for the pronominal status of the SM and OM is varied. Part of it is based on aspects of anaphoric binding, and part has its motivation in aspects of the phonology/syntax relation. The evidence based on anaphoric binding derives from differences between grammatical agreement and anaphoric relations. In general, grammatical agreement relations with non controlled arguments can be distinguished from anaphoric agreement relations by locality. Only anaphoric agreement relations can be non-local to the agreeing predicator. By "locality" is meant the proximity of the agreeing elements within clause structure; a local agreement relation is one which holds between elements of the same simple clause, while a non-local agreement relation is one which may hold between elements of different clauses. Noting that only grammatical functions that are governed by the predicator, such as SUBJ(ECT), OBJ(ECT), etc., can be in an agreement relation with it within a clause, the government relation between the predicator and its non-controlled arguments must be structurally local to the verb. On the other hand, an incorporated pronominal is a referential argument itself, governed by the verb. As such, an external referential noun phrase (NP) cannot also occupy the structural position of the pronominal argument or be related to that argument position by government. It can be related to it by anaphora with the agreeing incorporated pronoun. In general, anaphoric relations between (non-reflexive) pronouns and their antecedents are non-local to sentence structure, since their primary functions belong to discourse. Because only anaphoric agreement relation can be non-local to the agreeing predicator, the relation between the OM and the NP it agrees with is expected to be non-local, showing that it is indeed anaphoric agreement. This is shown in (6) below:

(6) a. Mikángó y-anú   anyaní   a-a-tsimikizil-á
        4-lions   4SM-your   2-baboons   2SM-perf-assure-fv
        njovu   kutí a-dzá-thá   ku-í-gúlíts-á kwá alenje.
        10-elephants that 2SM-fut-be able inf-sell-fv   to   2-hunters
        'Your lions, the baboons have assured the elephants that they (baboons) will
        be able to sell them (lions) to the hunters.'

    b. Mikángó i-ku-dzǐw-a   kutí njovu   zi-ku-fún-á   kutí
        4-lions   4SM-pres-know-fv that 10-elephants 10SM-pres-want-fv that
        anyaní   a-i-gúlíts-é   kwá alenje.
        2-baboons 2SM-4OM-sell-subjun to   2-hunters
        'The lions know that the elephants want the baboons to sell them (lions) to the
        hunters.'

The NP *mikángo* 'lions' can indeed be in a non-local relation with the predicator that has the OM, and yet be linked with it through anaphoric agreement relation. This shows that the OM is functioning as a pronominal argument and, as shown in (5g) above, the fact that the NPs can be omitted when the SM and OM are present indicates that the argument structure of the predicator is otherwise satisfied. In brief, the SM and OM satisfy the argument-structure requirements of the predicator, and the presence of the NPs is demanded by considerations extraneous to grammatical structure.

The pronominal argument status of the OM has been argued for a number of languages. In Kikuyu, it is noted that the OM and the overt nominal argument are in complementary distribution (Bergvall 1985, 1987; Mugane 1997). In Kinande, the presence of the OM is linked to left dislocation of the nominal phrase that it agrees with (Baker 2003; Mutaka 1995). A comparable analysis has been advanced for Kirundi (Sabimana 1986; Morimoto 2000) as well as Kihaya (Rubanza 1988). In brief, the presence of the OM has the effect of rendering the Nominal argument more of Topic than grammatical object. Baker (2003) notes for Kinande that agreement and dislocation go hand in hand. He notes, further, that "true polysynthetic languages like Mohawk are also consistent with this, in that they always have dislocation" (Baker 2003: 7). The idea is that discourse notions such as Topic or Focus normally occur on the periphery of the nuclear clause and the NP that agrees with the OM manifests the relevant distributional properties.

3.3   Phonological marking of the VP

The non-argument status of the NP in anaphoric agreement relation with the OM received further confirmation from tonal patterning in Chichewa. Bresnan and Mchombo (1987) noted that in Chichewa there are tonal changes that correlate with lengthening of the penultimate syllable in phrase-final position. In particular, final high tones retract to a low-toned penultimate syllable, yielding a rising tone. For instance, subjunctive -é has high tone when it is followed by an object of the subjunctive verb; but when the same verb is spoken in isolation or followed only by material that lies outside the verb phrase, such as a postposed subject NP, -é takes on a low tone, and the preceding syllable has a high or rising tone. The following examples illustrate the phenomenon:

(7)   Mikángó i-ku-fún-á   kutí anyaní   a-gwéts-é   miténgo.
       4-lions   4SM-pres-want-fv that 2-baboons 2SM-fell-subjun 4-trees
       'The lions want the baboons to cut down the trees.' (Lit.'The lions want that the baboons should fell the trees.')

In the example above, the high tone on the subjunctive -é is in anticipation of the object argument of the verb. Consider a verb that does not require an object argument.

(8)   Mikángó i-ku-fún-á   kutí anyaní   a-sěk-e   pa   chulu.
       4-lions   4SM-pres-want-fv that 2-baboons 2SM-laugh-subjun 16-loc 7-anthill
       'The lions want the baboons to laugh on the anthill.'

In the sentence above, the anthill is not an argument of the verb *seka* 'laugh.' It is a postverbal constituent that is not inside the verb phrase. The tone pattern seems to mark that. There is tonal retraction because *pa chulu* 'on the anthill' is not a postverbal constituent that is within the VP. Therefore, it does not prevent tonal retraction. On the other hand, when the OM appears in the verbal morphology, and the agreeing NP is present in the postverbal position, the tone marking is comparable to that of the marking of non-argument material.

(9)   Mikángó i-ku-fún-á   kutí anyaní   a-i-gwěts-e   miténgo.
       4-lions   4SM-pres-want-fv that 2-baboons 2SM-4OM-fell-subjun 4-trees
       'The lions want the baboons to cut them down (the trees).'(Lit. 'The lions want that the baboons should fell them (the trees).')

The subjunctive *-e* no longer has the high tone because the postverbal material, the NP agreeing with the OM, is regarded as not contained within the verb phrase. This is because the OM inside the verbal morphology satisfies the argument-structure requirements of the verb. A postverbal constituent inside the verb phrase prevents tonal retraction but those outside the VP do not.

3.4   The subject marker

There is an obvious asymmetry between the SM and OM. While the OM is not obligatory, the SM must be present. Such obligatoriness is characteristic of grammatical agreement. Should the SM be analyzed as an incorporated pronominal argument too? The SM has indeed received varying analyses in Bantu linguistics (Demuth and Johnson 1989; Marten 1999; Morimoto 2002; Sabimana 1986). On the one hand, the SM allows for non-local relation between the predicator and the NP, comparable to the anaphoric agreement relation between the OM and the agreeing NP. Consider sentence (10) below:

(10)   Mikángó i-ku-dziw-a   kuti njovu   zi-ku-fun-a   kuti
        4-lions   4SM-pres-know-fv that 10-elephants 10SM-pres-want-fv that
        i-thamangits-e   anyani.
        4SM-chase-subjun 2-baboons
        'The lions know that the elephants want them to chase the baboons.' (Lit. 'The
        lions know that the elephants want that they (lions) should chase the baboons.')

The fact that the verb *thamangitsa* 'chase,' appearing here in the subjunctive form as *thamangitse*, is construed as having *mikángo* 'lions' for its subject derives from the relation between the nominal *mikángo* and the SM. Note that *mikángo* is in a different clause. This makes the status of SM comparable to that of the OM. However, the SM is obligatory and other Bantu languages, for instance Kinande (cf. Baker 2003), seem to require proximity between the verb and the NP that the SM agrees with. Bresnan and Mchombo (1986, 1987) analyzed the SM as functionally ambiguous between an agreement marker and an incorporated pronominal argument. When the SM is used as a grammatical agreement marker, it agrees with a nominal that has the Subject function; when the SM is used for anaphoric binding, its antecedent within the sentence has the Topic (TOP) function. The TOP in this case can be analyzed as a grammaticized topic. Grammatical theory has to provide for the separation of such argument functions as SUBJ(ECT), OBJ(ECT), OBL(IQUE), from non-argument functions like TOP, FOC(US), and ADJ(UNCT).

The complications for the status of the SM come from the fact that it has to be marked on nominal modifiers within the NP, as well as in constructions where its status as a pronominal marker could be questioned. In order to show its involvement in grammatical agreement, we will consider the structure of the noun phrase.

3.5   The noun phrase

Chichewa is a strictly head-initial language. Within the noun phrase, the head noun precedes its complements. The internal organization of the NP can be illustrated by the following:

(11) a.   Noun + Dem   mikángó iyo   'those lions'
     b.   Noun + Num   mikángó i-tátu   'three lions'
     c.   Noun + Assoc+Noun   mikángó yá úlemu   'lions of respect'
     d.   Noun + Assoc+inf-Verb   mikángó yó-sautsa   'bothersome lions'
     e.   Noun + Relative clause   mikángó i-méné í-ku-sáutsa   'lions which bother'
     f.   Noun + Poss   mikángó y-âthu   'our lions'
     g.   Noun + Adjective stem   mikángó yáíkúlu   'big lions'

There are very few 'pure' adjective stems in Chichewa. These are identified by the fact that they take double prefixation. Essentially, the noun-class marker is prefixed to the adjective stem first, then the associative marker is added to which the class marker is re-attached. The example in (11g) illustrates the point. The adjective stem is -kúlu 'big.' To this the class marker [i] for class 4 which has mikángo 'lions' is prefixed, yielding ikulu. Then the associative marker -a is attached, to which the class marker is prefixed again. The full set of such adjective stems is provided below:

-muna   'male'
-kazi   'female'
-ng'ono   'small'
-kulu   'big'
-wisi   'unripe'
-kali   'fierce, ferocious'
-fupi   'short'
-tali   'long, tall'
-nyinji   'plenty, many'

The combination of the SM i with the associative marker -a- is phonologically realized as ya, and of u and -a is realized as wa. A more intricately organized NP can be demonstrated by the following:

(12)   Mikángó y-anú   i-tátu   iyi   i-méné í-ku-sáuts-á   alenje . . .
        4-lions 4SM-your 4SM-three 4dem   4SM-rel 4SM-pres-bother-fv 2-hunters
        'These three lions of yours which are bothering the hunters . . .'

The ordering of the constituents of the NP is subject to variation, correlating with discourse effects. The NP *mikángó i-tátu iyi* 'these three lions' could also come out as *mikángó iyi itátu*. These examples illustrate that within the NP, complements of the head noun must agree with it. This is irrespective of the grammatical function associated with the NP. Thus, if the NP in (12) were to function as the grammatical object of the verb, the agreement pattern within it would still have to hold. This is shown in (13):

(13)   Asodzi   a-dzá-bá   mikángó yanú . . .
        2-fishermen 2SM-fut-steal 4-lions   4SMyour . . .
        'The fishermen will steal these three lions of yours . . .'

In light of its obligatory presence even in cases where its status as a pronominal argument is in doubt, the question persists as to the proper analysis of the SM. This is made more evident by other issues surrounding the SM, which we shall now consider.

The status of the SM has been controversial for a number of reasons. As noted, the obligatory occurrence of the SM has been taken as grounds for analyzing it as an agreement marker suggesting, as indicated above, that the nominal expression that agrees with it must be the subject of the sentence. This has been compounded by notable differences between the relation holding between the SM and the agreed-with nominal and that between the OM and the nominal it agrees with. For instance, Baker (2003) has noted that in Kinande, a left-dislocated object is indeed a topic in that it must be set apart from the rest of the sentence by a clear intonation break. Also, it must come before the preverbal subject in a sentence that has both. Further, it can come before a focused NP but never after it. Preverbal subjects show the opposite distribution.

The SM has also been observed to serve a variety of functions. In languages with object–subject reversal, the SM agrees with the object nominal although the reading suggests otherwise (Morimoto 2002). This is exemplified by the following, from Kinyarwanda:

(14) a.   Umuhuungu a-ra-som-a   igitabo.
           1-boy   1-pres-read-asp 7-book
           'The boy is reading the book.'

     b.   Igitabo ki-som-a   umuhuungu.
           7-book 7SM-pres-read-asp 1-boy
           'The book is being read by the boys.' (Lit. 'The book is reading the boy.')

In Kinyarwanda, the subject–object reversal constructions are, apparently, "often translated as either cleft or passive" (Morimoto 2002: 4). From these observations Morimoto concludes that the SM is really a topic marker. The difference between the topic marked by the SM and that marked by the OM is dealt with by making a distinction between an internal topic and an external topic.

In locative inversion constructions in Chichewa the SM agrees with the preverbal locative nominal (Bresnan 1994; Bresnan and Kanerva 1989), as in the following examples:

(15) a.   Pa   mudzí   pá-dá-gw-á   njala.
           16-loc 3-village 16SM-pst-fall-fv 9-hunger
           'Famine ravaged the land.' (Lit. 'In the village fell hunger (famine).')

In these examples there is evidence that the postverbal NP is construed as the subject, despite its lack of agreement with the SM. In fact, in these constructions the postverbal NP lacks the canonical properties of objecthood. For instance, it cannot be marked by an OM. Sentence (15b) below, in which there is an OM agreeing with *njala* 'hunger,' is ungrammatical:

    b.   *Pa   mudzí   pá-dá-í-gw-a   njala
           16-loc 3-village 16SM-pst-9OM-fall-fv 9-hunger

This could be a consequence of the fact that the verb *gwa* 'fall' is intransitive, raising further the question of how to construe the postverbal nominal. Note that transitive verbs do not allow locative inversion, except when they have been passivized (cf. Bresnan and Kanerva 1989, 1992). In addition, it is noted by Bresnan (1994), citing Katupha, that in Makua (P30 according to Guthrie's classification), a language spoken in parts of southern Tanzania and northern Mozambique, there is optional object marking of a class 1 subject that has undergone locative inversion.

Further complications regarding the SM arise in constructions with conjoined NPs in subject or object position. Since nouns in Bantu languages belong to different gender classes, when there is co-ordination of nouns from different noun classes, there is the question of how the shape or form of the SM is to be determined. What does the SM really encode? In a study of agreement in conjoined noun phrases in Swahili, Marten (1999) concludes that the SM has various functions in that it marks morphological agreement in some cases, it is in anaphoric agreement with the co-ordinate NP in others, and in yet other cases it marks syntactic agreement. The different analyses of the SM have, naturally, led to divergent views about its role in Bantu languages (cf. Corbett and Mtenje 1987; Mchombo and Ngunga 1994; Reynolds and Eastman 1989). For Chichewa the standard view that the SM is functionally ambiguous between agreement marker and incorporated pronominal will be taken as a first approximation in this work. In this regard, the analysis of the SM and OM as incorporated pronominal arguments assimilates the structure of Chichewa to the pronominal argument hypothesis proposed by Jelinek (1984) for polysynthetic languages; Jelinek's study is reviewed and commented upon further in work by Austin and Bresnan (1996). This will be taken up later. In line with the pronominal argument hypothesis it will be maintained that the SM does function as a pronominal subject argument within the verbal morphology. It remains functionally ambiguous retaining the status of an agreement marker too.

In this respect the analysis offered for Chichewa will be comparable to that proposed for Setawana by Demuth and Johnson (1989) or Kirundi by Sabimana (1986). For Setawana, Demuth and Johnson argue that the SM is the subject and the OM is the object in comparable constructions in that language. The difference between the SM in Chichewa and in Setawana is that in the former the SM maintains the functional ambiguity of being partially an agreement marker, hence it is not always pronominal, while in Setawana the SM is always pronominal. The nominal expressions are effectively adjuncts bearing discourse functions.

3.6   Complementation

One significant aspect of clause structure is complementation. Complement clauses function as arguments or dependents of head nouns or verbs. Within NPs the commonest clausal complement is the relative clause. This will be taken up below. At this juncture, attention will be on verb complements.

In Chichewa verbal complements are either object NPs, infinitival constructions, or embedded sentences introduced by the complementizer *kutí* 'that.' These are shown below:

(16) a.   Anyaní   a-ku-b-á   mikánda.
      2-baboons 2SM-pres-steal-fv 4-beads
      'The baboons are stealing some beads.'

    b.   Anyaní   a-ku-fún-á   ku-b-á   mikánda.
      2-baboons 2SM-pres-want-fv inf-steal-fv 4-beads
      'The baboons want to steal some beads.'

    c.   Anyaní   a-ku-fún-á   kutí njovu   zi-b-é   mikánda.
      2-baboons 2SM-pres-want-fv that 10-elephants 10SM-steal-subjun 4-beads
      'The baboons want the elephants to steal some beads.'

    d.   Anyaní   a-ku-phúnzíts-á   mikángó ku-b-á   mikánda.
      2-baboons 2SM-pres-teach-fv 4-lions   inf-steal-fv 4-beads
      'The baboons are teaching lions (how) to steal beads.'

Infinitival complements can readily be subsumed to Control constructions. The infinitival complement has a SUBJ missing, and that missing SUBJ is construed with either the SUBJ or OBJ of the matrix clause. The general strategy is for the missing subject to be construed with the OBJ of the matrix clause if there is one, otherwise with the SUBJ (cf. Brame 1976; Bresnan 1982a; Chomsky 1980, 1981; Horrocks 1987; Koster and May 1982; Mchombo and Mtenje 1983; Sells 1985). Infinitival complements in Chichewa are less common than embedded clauses which get introduced by the complementizer *kutí* 'that' and retain the subject NP or the SM. The complement clause can be just like the matrix clause with some verbs such as think, know, etc., or may be in the subjunctive mood, traditionally indicated by the change of the final vowel -a of the verb to -e. This is illustrated in sentence (16c) above. Embedded clauses display characteristics that distinguish them from matrix clauses. For a start, the verb does not inflect for tense/aspect, obvious in the case of infinitival clauses. There may appear to be an exception with the future marker. Note the following:

(17) a.   Anyaní   a-ku-fún-á   kutí mikángó i-dzá-b-é   mikánda.
          2-baboons 2SM-pres-want-fv that 4-lions   4SM-fut-steal-subjun 4-beads
          'The baboons want the lions to steal (at a future date) some beads.'

   b. *Anyaní   a-ku-fún-á   kutí mikángó i-ku-b-é   mikánda.
          2-baboons 2SM-pres-want-fv that 4-lions   4SM-pres-steal-subjun 4-beads

Sentence (17b) is ungrammatical because the subjunctive verb has a present-tense marker. The problem with the future-tense marker is that it is formally identical with the directional marker -dza- which derives from the verb -dza 'come.' This directional marker, conveying the reading of 'come and do something' contrasts with the other directional marker -ka- conveying the reading of 'go and do something.' This latter derives from the verb -muka or -mka 'go.' This verb only survives in some dialects, having been virtually replaced by the verb -pita 'go.' The verb -dza is also less commonly used, having been overtaken by the verb -bwela 'come.' These two directional markers are attached after the tense/aspect marker in the verbal morphology. Consider the following:

(18) a.   Anyaní   a-ku-ká-b-á   mikánda.
          2-baboons 2SM-pres-dir-steal-fv 4-beads
          'The baboons are going to steal some beads.'

   b.   Anyaní   a-ku-dzá-b-á   mikánda.
          2-baboons 2SM-pres-dir-steal-fv 4-beads
          'The baboons are coming to steal some beads.'

It is arguable that the future-tense marker -dza- in Chichewa is not distinguishable from the directional marker. In fact, the two do not co-occur. Thus, while sentence (18b) illustrates the co-occurrence of the directional marker -dza- with the present-tense marker -ku-, sentence (18c) shows that the future-tense marker fails to co-occur with the directional marker.

   c. *Anyaní   a-dza-dzá-b-á   mikánda.
          2-baboons 2SM-fut-dir-steal-fv 4-beads
          'The baboons will come to steal some beads.'

That may account for the fact that -dza- can appear with the subjunctive since directional markers can be attached to verbs in the subjunctive mood.

(19) a. Njuchí zi-a-lamul-a   kutí anyaní   a-ká-b-é   mikánda.
         10-bees 10SM-perf-order-fv that 2-baboons 2SM-dir-steal-subjun 4-beads
         'The bees have ordered that the baboons should go and steal some beads.'

   b.   Njuchí zi-a-lamul-a   kutí anyaní   a-dzá-dy-é   ŭchi.
        10-bees 10SM-perf-order-fv that 2-baboons 2SM-dir-eat-subjun 14-honey
        'The bees have ordered that the baboons should come and eat the honey.'

Note, further, that the directional markers can appear with infinitival constructions, yet tense/aspect markers do not, with the exception of the habitual marker *-ma-*.

   c.   Anyaní   a-ku-fúná   ku-ká-b-á   mikánda.
        2-baboons 2SM-pres-want-fv inf-dir-steal-fv 4-beads
        'The baboons want to go and steal some beads.'

   d.   Anyaní   a-ku-fúná   ku-dzá-b-á   mikánda.
        2-baboons 2SM-pres-want-fv inf-dir-steal-fv 4-beads
        'The baboons want to come and steal some beads.'

Another feature of the embedded clause in the subjunctive mood has to do with negation. The negative marker in the matrix clause is *si-* and it is prefixed to the SM. In other words, it is the first proclitic in the verbal morphology. This is illustrated in the following sentence:

(20)   Anyaní   sí-á-ku-dzá-ngó-b-á   mikánda, a-ku-dzá-b-á-nsó
       2-baboons neg-2SM-pres-dir-just-steal-fv 4-beads   2SM-pres-dir-steal-fv-also
       chímánga.
       7-corn
       'The baboons are not just coming to steal some beads, they are coming to steal
       corn as well.'

In the embedded clause, both infinitival and subjunctive, the negative marker is *-sa-* and it is placed after the infinitive marker, in infinitival constructions, and after the SM in subjunctive clauses:

(21) a. Alenje   a-ku-dzíw-á   kutí ku-sa-phunzíl-a kú-ma-dzéts-á
         2-hunters 2SM-pres-know-fv that inf-neg-learn-fv 15SM-hab-bring-fv
         chisokonezo.
         7-confusion
         'The hunters know that lack of education (Lit. not learning) brings confusion.'

   b.   Asodzi   a-da-lámúl-á   kutí alenje   a-sa-uz-ídw-é   zá
        2-fishermen 2SM-pst-order-fv that 2-hunters 2SM-neg-tell-pass-subjun about
        chiwembú chá   mikángo.
        7-plot   7SM-assoc 4-lions
        'The fishermen ordered that the hunters should not be told about the
        conspiracy of the lions.'

The distribution of the negative markers and inflection for tense/aspect are among features that correlate with matrix versus complement clause distinction.

There are other constructions that seem to require subjunctive constructions. The next section will describe some of them. There is no theoretical issue involved with these elements, although they will be relevant to discussion of verbal morphology in general.

3.7   The modals *-nga-* 'can, may,' *-ngo-* 'just,' *-zi-* 'compulsive,' and *-ba-* 'continuative'

There is a modal element *-nga-* with a reading of 'can or may.' It appears after the SM and has the distribution of tense/aspect. Tense markers do not co-occur with this modal element. When it appears, the verb must be in the subjunctive. Consider the following:

(22)   Mu-nga-ndí-thándiz-e.
2nd pl-mod-1st sing-help-subjun
'You can/may help me.'

There is another modal, *-ngo-* with the reading of 'just.' This one does not appear with the subjunctive. It is normally placed just before the OM in the verbal morphology, and after all the other verbal proclitics.

(23)   Mkángo u-ku-ngó-zí-námĭz-a   njovu.
3-lion   3SM-pres-mod-1OOM-deceive-fv 10-elephants
'The lion is merely (just) deceiving the elephants.'

When the two modals appear together within the verbal morphology, the verb cannot be in the subjunctive.

(24)   Mu-nga-ngo-ndí-páts-á   tsoka.
2nd pl-can-just-1st sing-give-fv 5-misfortune
'You may just give me bad luck.' ('Lest you just give me bad luck.')

The two modals can appear with the directional elements *-ka-* and *-dza-*, as shown below:

(25) a.   Mu-nga-ka-mù-th-ets-el-é   ukwati.
2nd pl-may-dir-3rd sing-end-caus-appl-subjun 14-marriage
'Lest you go and end his marriage for him.'

   b.   Mu-ká-ngó-mú-th-éts-él-a   ukwati.
2nd pl-dir-just-3rd sing-end-caus-appl-fv 14-marriage
'Just go and end his marriage for him.'

Sometimes when the modal *-nga-* appears with a directional marker, the latter appears in a verb that is complement to the verb *-tha* 'finish, end, be able to, can' to which -*nga*- is attached. This is illustrated in the following:

(26)   Mu-nga-th-e   ku-ká-b-á   mikánda.
         2nd pl-can-able-subjun   inf-dir-steal-fv 4-beads
         'You can go and steal the beads.'

Although the modal -*nga*- requires the subjunctive form, the subjunctive is not
really used as complement to a matrix verb. It highlights uses of the subjunctive
as what has been termed 'polite imperative.' This will be discussed in the next
section.

There is another modal element -*zi*- that has the reading of 'must' or 'should.'
It can be viewed as conveying the sense of compulsion or obligation. Like -*nga*- it
appears in the tense/aspect position, and after the SM. As such, it does not co-occur
with tense/aspect. Further, it has a habitual reading in that it conveys the meaning
of being obligated to do something regularly. Thus it could be characterized as
saying that one should be doing something as a regular assignment or as part of
normal living. This modal can co-occur with all the pre-verb-stem elements that
come after the tense/aspect marker slot, but it does not occur with the verb in the
subjunctive.

(27) a.   Mkángo   u-zí-b-á   mikánda.
          3-lion   3SM-must-steal-fv   4-beads
          'The lion must (should) steal beads.'

     b.   Mkángo   u-zí-ká-b-á   mikánda.
          3-lion   3SM-must dir-steal-fv   4-beads
          'The lion must go and steal beads.'

     c.   Mkángo   u-zí-ngó-b-á   mikánda.
          3-lion   3SM-must-just-steal-fv   4-beads
          'The lion must only steal beads.'

     d.   Mkángo   u-zí-ká-ngó-b-á   mikánda.
          3-lion   3SM-must-dir-just-steal-fv   4-beads
          'The lion must go and steal beads only.'

     e.   Mkángo   u-zí-ká-ngó-wá-dy-éts-á   nyêmba   anyǎni.
          3-lion   3SM-must-dir-just-2OM-eat-caus-fv   10-beans 2-baboons
          'The lion must go and feed the baboons only beans.'

However, note that when the verb is in the subjunctive, the sentence with this
modal is ungrammatical.

     f.   *Mkángo   u-zí-b-é   mikánda.
           3-lion   3SM-must-steal-subjun 4-beads

Another element to be considered here is -*ba*-. This conveys the idea of 'continuing to do something.' It does not appear with the subjunctive. Further, although
it does co-occur with a tense marker, it seems to require the present tense only,

for those speakers who can have the two together. This may be a consequence of the fact it has the discourse function of encoding the continuation of an activity already in progress. The following provide useful examples:

(28) a. Inu   tsogolani ine   ndí-bá-malíz-á   nchíto-yi.
        2nd pl go ahead   1st sing 1st sing-cont-complete-fv 9-job-proxdem
        'As for you, go ahead, while I (continue to) complete this job.'

The element -ba- does not readily co-occur with the other modals indicated above. Some speakers seem to tolerate the co-occurrence of -ba- with -ngo-, as in the sentence below:

   b. Mikángó i-bá-ngo-sák-á   mbîdzi.
      4-lions   4SM-cont-just-hunt-fv 10-zebras
      'The lions should just continue to hunt zebras.'

For those speakers who can combine this element with the present tense, the relevant example is provided by the following:

   c. Mikángó i-ku-bá-ngo-sák-á   mbîdzi.
      4-lions   4SM-pres-cont-just-hunt-fv 10-zebras
      'The lions are just continuing to hunt the zebras.'

3.8   -sana- 'before' and -kana- 'would have'

There is a form *sana* meaning 'before' which appears in the verbal morphology. The appearance of -sana- always requires the subjunctive form and it appears after the SM. One significant feature of this element, like the other one to be discussed in this section, is that it comprises two syllables. The two components do not readily lend themselves to morphological analysis. In brief, the two syllables cannot be correlated with separate morphemes. This is illustrated by the following:

(29) a. Mkángó ú-sáná-b-é   míkánda, u-na-mw-á   mowa.
        3-lion   3SM-before-steal-subjun 4-beads   3SM-pst-drink 3-beer
        'Before the lion stole the beads, it drank beer.'

The ordering of the 'before-clause' with respect to the main clause can be the other way round.

   b. Mkángó u-na-mw-á   mowa ú-sáná-b-é   mikánda.
      3-lion   3SM-pst-drink-fv 3-beer 3SM-before-steal-subjun 4-beads
      'The lion drank beer before it stole the beads.'

Another element that, like -sana-, also consists of two syllables is -kana-. This seems to be the limit of their similarity. The latter, which has a conditional reading as well as the reading of 'would have,' does not appear in the subjunctive. The two readings indicated above are separated by different tonal patterns. Note the following:

(30) a.   Mkángó ú-kána-b-á   mikánda, u-kaná-sángálala.
          3-lion   3SM-cond-steal-fv 4-beads   3SM-would have-rejoice
          'Had the lion stolen the beads, it would have been very happy.'

While -sana- does not readily co-occur with other modal elements, -kana- can combine with -ngo-. This is illustrated below:

   b.   Mkángó ú-kána-ngó-b-á   mikánda, u-kaná-íiıb-ídw-á
        3-lion   3SM-cond-just-steal-fv 4-bead   3SM-would have-sing-pass-fv
        mlăndu.
        3-case
        'Had the lion just stolen the beads, it would have been prosecuted.'

It seems that -kana-, unlike -sana-, appears to comprise two morphemes, the conditional -ka- and the past-tense morpheme -na-. This is evident from the dialectal variation form of -kada- where -da- is an allomorph of the past-tense morpheme. The tones remain unchanged. There is another usage of -kana-, tonally different from the former, that has the reading of 'to still be doing something.' This is exemplified by the following:

   c.   Mkángó u-kana-sáká   mbĭdzi.
        3-lion   3SM-still-hunt 10-zebras
        'The lion is still hunting zebras.'

In this usage, -kana- or -kada- is low-toned.

3.9   The imperative

The imperative in Chichewa comes in two forms. The first involves the simple use of the bare verb stem. This can be gleaned from the data below:

(31)   Gŏna!   'Lie down, sleep!'
        Luma!   'Bite!'
        Thamănga!   'Run!'
        Seka!   'Laugh!'

The imperative requires satisfaction of the minimality condition in that the verb stem must consist of a foot. In the case of monosyllabic verb stems, such as -ba 'steal,' the minimality condition is satisfied through the prefixation of the vowel i- to the verb. This yields the form iba 'steal.' When the command is issued to more than one individual, then an enclitic ni, which is part of the object form for the second person plural, is added. The second-person pronoun, when it occurs as a grammatical object, is realized by -*ku*- in its singular form. As with other OMs, it appears in the immediate pre-verb-stem position, the normal position for the OM.

(32) a.   Mkángó   ú-ma-ku-kónd-a
          3-lion   3SM-hab-2[nd]singOM-love-fv
          'The lion loves you.'

In the case of the second person plural, the object form is realized by the discontinuous form -*ku* . . . *ni*, flanking the verb.

   b.   Mkángó   ú-ma-ku-kónd-a-ni.
        3-lion   3SM-hab-2nd plOM-love-fv-2nd pl
        'The lion loves you.'

The second person plural is also used for politeness or formality in ordinary usage. The -*ni* that comprises the second part of the discontinuous object form of the second person plural is what is used in imperatives. Thus, the imperatives in (31) have, as their plural counterparts, the following:

(33)   Gonáni!   'Lie down, sleep!'
          Lumani!   'Bite!'
          Thamangáni!   'Run!'
          Sekani!   'Laugh!'

The above examples involve intransitive verbs. With transitive verbs, the bare imperatives can be used when the object is a full NP, not a pronominal.

(34) a.   Gumulaní   zisakasa!
          pull down 8-huts
          'Pull down (demolish) the huts!'

   b.   Manganí   mikéka!
        tie up   4-mats
        'Tie up the mats!'

The negative form of these bare imperatives uses a special element *osa* which is prefixed to the verb stem. It also neutralizes the singular and plural distinction. Thus the negative imperatives of these forms are:

   c.   Ósagóna!   'Do not lie down, do not sleep!'
        Ósamángá mikéka! 'Do not tie up the mats!'
        Ósa-i-măng-a!   'Do not tie them up!'

The negative imperative, unlike the affirmative, can take a pronominal object, as shown in the previous example. In the affirmative, the bare imperative form does not take a pronominal object. Instead, the verb must be in the subjunctive mood, as shown below:

d. Zi-gúmúl-é-(ni)!
    1OOM-pull down-subjun-(2nd pl)
    'Pull them down!'

Alternatively, the SM can also be used:

e. Mu-zi-gúmúl-e!
    2nd pl-8OM-pull down-subjun
    'You should pull them down!'

The negative of these forms exploits the negative marker *-sa-* used with the subjunctive, indicating its status as a complement clause.

f. Mu-sa-zi-gumúl-e!
    2nd pl-neg-8OM-pull down-subjun
    'Do not pull them down!'

The subjunctive form is also used when directional markers are present, but without the modal *-ngo-*. Consider the following examples:

(35) a. Ka-i-mángé-(ni)!
         dir-4OM-tie up-subjun-(2nd pl)
         'Go and tie them (mats) up!'

The negative always uses the other form with the SM:

b. Mu-sa-ka-i-máng-e.
    2nd pl-neg-dir-4OM-tie up-subjun
    'Do not go and tie them up!'

As indicated above, the modal *-ngo-* does not appear with the subjunctive form. Even in imperatives, when *-ngo-* is used, the subjunctive form disappears.

(36) a. Mu-ká-ngó-zí-gúmul-a!
         2nd pl-dir-just-8OM-pull down-fv
         'Just go and pull them down!'

Curiously, the negative of this form employs the *-sa-* normally used in the subjunctive.

b. Mu-sa-ká-ngó-zí-gúmŭl-a.
    2nd pl-neg-dir-just-8OM-pull-down-fv
    'Don't just go and pull them down.'

The modal *-nga-*, on the other hand, although it normally requires the subjunctive, unless the modal *-ngo-* is present, does not use the negation ordinarily found with the subjunctive. Instead, it is negated with the negative marker *si-* used in matrix clauses. This is illustrated in (37) below:

(37) a. Mu-nga-ndí-páts-é   tsoka.
         2nd pl-may-1st sing-give-subjun   5-misfortune
         'You may give me bad luck.' ('Lest you give me bad luck.')

    b.   Sí-mú-nga-ndi-páts-é   tsoka.
         neg-2nd pl-can-1st sing-give-subjun   5-misfortune
         'You cannot give me bad luck.'

The interaction between negation and modals clearly deserves more investigation than it is likely to receive in this work.

3.10   The imperative with *ta-*

The bare stem imperative does not take a pronominal object, as noted above. When there is a pronominal object the subjunctive form is used. There is, however, another proclitic *ta-* which appears after the SM and is used in the sense of imploring someone to do something. This morpheme *-ta-* is low-toned, to be distinguished from a high-toned *-tá-* that is used to mark series of events in sequential arrangement. This is illustrated by the following:

(38) Mkángo u-ná-b-á   mikánda. Ú-tá-í-b-a,   u-na-pít-á
      3-lion   3SM-pst-steal-fv   4-beads   3SM-after-4OM-steal-fv 3SM-pst-go-fv
      ku   thengo ku-ká-úz-á   anyáni   zá   ukatswílí w-áke.
      17-loc 5-bush inf-dir-tell-fv 2-baboons about 14-skills 14SM-his
      'The lion stole some beads. After stealing them (having stolen them), he went into the bush to tell the baboons about his skills.'

The *-ta-* illustrated above is different from the other *-ta-*. This latter is shown in the following examples:

(39) a. Mu-ta-ndí-thándĭz-a . . .
         2nd pl-impl-1st sing-help-fv
         'Could you help me . . .'

As shown, it, too, does appear after the SM and in the position traditionally occupied by the tense/aspect. However, this *-ta-* can also be used to give instructions, with the sense of imploring someone to do something. When used as such, it takes the pronominal object but it does not appear with the verb in the subjunctive. Consider the following examples:

    b.   Ta-zím-á-(ni)   móto.
         impl-put out-fv-(2nd pl)   3-fire
         'Could you (kindly) put out (extinguish) the fire.'

    c.   Ta-ú-zím-ǎ-(ni).
         impl-3OM-extinguish-fv-(2nd pl)
         'Kindly extinguish it (fire).'

To negate this form, either one of the negatives mentioned above is used. One can use the negative with *ósá* to give *ósá-u-zǐma* 'do not put it out.' Alternatively, the form with -*sa*- in the subjunctive can be used, as in *mu-sa-u-zǐm-e* 'do not extinguish it.'

3.11   Conditional -*ka*-

One more morpheme that occurs in the tense/aspect position is the conditional -*ka*-, and it is low-toned. This is shown in the following example:

(40)   Mkángo u-ka-b-á   mikánda akází   a-dzá-zúnzǐk-a.
        3-lion   3SM-cond-steal-fv 4-beads 2-women 2SM-fut-suffer-fv
        'If the lion steals the beads, the women will suffer.'

This conditional does not have a negative form. To get a negative conditional, the word *ngati* 'if' is used. Constructions with *ngati* provide an alternative to forming conditionals.

(41)   Ngati mkángo ú-b-á   mikánda akází   a-dzá-zúnzǐk-a.
        if   3-lion   3SM-steal-fv   4-beads 2-women 2SM-fut-suffer-fv
        'If the lion steals the beads, the women will suffer.'

The sentence with *ngati* 'if' can then be negated. This is illustrated by the sentence below:

(42)   Ngati mkángo si-u-dzá-b-á   mikánda amúná a-dzá-sángálal-a.
        if   3-lion   neg-3SM-fut-steal-fv   4-beads 2-men 2SM-fut-be happy-fv
        'If the lion will not steal the beads, the men will be very happy.'

The discussion above indicates that within the verbal morphology in Chichewa, the post-subject-marker position can be occupied by tense/aspect markers, the modals -*nga*- and -*zi*-, the negative marker -*sa*-, normally occurring with the verb in the subjunctive, the -*ta*- indicating request or imploring, or the -*tá*- used to mark the sequence of events. The general template seems to be as follows, in order of appearance:

NEG (si)
subject marker
{T/A, NEG (sa), MOD (-nga-, -zi-, -ta-, -ba-)
CONDITIONAL -ka-
DIRECTIONAL (-ká-, -dza-)
MOD (-ngo-)
object marker
verb stem

The ordering of these pre-verb-stem elements probably has theoretical significance. Certainly the rigidity of the ordering and the functional aspects of these morphemes have consequences on their analysis. It will be noted that while the pre-verb-stem morphemes are more oriented towards aspects of clause structure and are fixed in their order, verbal suffixes are formally and functionally different. The latter are involved in aspects of argument structure and, within limits, there is some variability in their ordering relations. These considerations make for a principled demarcation of the morphology within the verb stem, and the linguistic processes that occur therein. In brief, the morphological organization of the verbal unit in Chichewa shows that there is a division or partitioning within it. There is a substructure, the verb stem, which is the domain of argument-structure-changing morphology. This unit has lexical integrity that is manifested by the fact that it is the domain of a number of significant linguistic processes. These will be commented upon later. Note that verb-stem morphotactics will differ from those constraining the pre-verb-stem elements. Further, while the verb stem is the domain of lexical operations, the pre-verb-stem morphemes are relevant to clause structure. The verbal morphology in Chichewa provides ground for the separation of derivational morphology from inflectional morphology. Henceforth, it will be maintained that the pre-verb-stem elements are clitics. More on this later (see chapter 5).

3.12   Conclusion

In this chapter attention was focused on aspects of complementation. While there was discussion of nominal complementation, the greater part of the chapter has been devoted to verbal complementation and the issues arising from that. There has been some discussion of the elements that appear prefixed to the verb stem, their interaction with forms of clauses, as well as their general ordering restrictions. It has been noted that the morphemes that will be termed clitics have a fairly rigid ordering pattern. In this respect, they are shown to differ from verbal extensions, both formally and functionally. The latter affect argument structure and, subject to either syntactic derivation or semantic scope requirements, their ordering relations may allow for variability. The verb stem is the domain of lexical operations and the clitics are relevant to clause structure. In the next chapter, we will take another look at nominal complementation, especially relative-clause formation. This will be connected to discussion of other aspects of clause structure, specifically, cleft constructions and question formation.

4

Relative clauses, clefts, and question formation

4.1   Relative-clause formation

The discussion in the preceding chapter concentrated on verbal complementation with some remarks on the structure of the noun phrase. The noun phrase also provides instances of complementation with a nominal head. It has been indicated that within the noun phrase modifiers of the head noun are marked for agreement with that noun, in number and gender. In this chapter attention will turn to the relative clause. The relative clause provides the easiest form of clausal complementation to a nominal head. It also gives variations that are of intrinsic interest to theoretical discussion (cf. Biloa 1990; Chomsky 1977; Keach 1980; Ngonyani 1998b). However, before focusing on the relative construction, comment should be made on non-relative complements. These would be of the variety exemplified in English by expressions such as 'the belief that it would rain.' In Chichewa such complementation is achieved by the use of the verb *tí* 'say' in its infinitive form *kutí* 'that,' linked to the head noun by the associative marker *-á*. For most speakers the sequence *á* + *kutî* is reduced to *otí*. Ordinarily, the coalescence of the associative marker *á* with the infinitive marker *ku* to *o* is sensitive to the syllable structure of the ensuing verb. It is possible when the verb is not monosyllabic. This is one of the cases when the sensitivity to syllable structure is over-ridden, generally characteristic of some dialects of Chichewa, such as the dialect described by Mark Hanna Watkins (1937). The nominal complementation is illustrated by the following examples:

(1) a.   Chiyembekezo ch-otí   anyaní   a-dzá-bwél-á   ndí míkánda
          7-expectation   7SM-assoc-that 2-baboons 2SM-fut-come-fv with 4-beads
          'The expectation that the baboons will come with (some) beads'

   b.   Maganizo otí   akaídí   a-zí-dy-á   mbewa
          6-thought 6SM-assoc-that 2-prisoners 2SM-must-eat-fv 10-mice
          a-a-sek-ets-á   alenje.
          6SM-perf-laugh-caus-fv 2-hunters
          'The suggestion that prisoners (should) must eat mice has made the hunters laugh.'

Although in the sections that follow attention will focus on relative-clause formation, the nominal complementation illustrated here should be kept in mind. There may be further comment on it when need arises.

4.2   Relativization in Chichewa

The relative construction in Chichewa comes in two forms. The first one employs a relative marker -méne 'that,' which introduces the relative clause. This has a variant -omwe (with an allomorph -emwe). The other form of the relative clause uses an invariant -o. This is suffixed to the verb and prefixed with a marker for agreement with the relativized head noun. The invariant -o can be taken to be comparable to that used in the related language of Swahili. Ashton (1947) referred to that one as the 'o-' of reference (cf. Ngonyani 1998b). The latter strategy for relativization will be discussed later. We will begin with the relative-clause formation that is more transparent in its illustration of complementation to a nominal head.

4.3   The relative marker -mene

The relative clause in Chichewa is comparable to relative-clause construction in English. The relativized head noun appears initially within the NP configuration. The relative clause is introduced by the marker -méne. To this relative marker is prefixed the class marker for the head noun. This is illustrated in the sentences below:

(2) a.   Anyaní   a-ku-b-á   míkánda.
          2-baboons 2SM-pres-steal-fv 4-beads
          'The baboons are stealing beads.'

    b.   Anyaní   a-méné á-kú-b-á   míkánda a-ku-dz-éts-á
          2-baboons 2SM-rel 2SM-pres-steal-fv 4-beads 2SM-pres-come-caus-fv
          chisokonezo.
          7-confusion
          'The baboons that are stealing beads are bringing confusion.'

    c.   Mikándá i-méné anyaní   á-kǔ-b-a   ndi y-a
          4-beads 4SM-rel 2-baboons 2SM-pres-steal-fv be   4SM-assoc
          akází   a-á   ku   Mangochi.
          2-women 2SM-assoc 17-loc Mangochi
          'The beads that the baboons are stealing belong to the women from Mangochi.'

Note that both the subject NP and the object NP can be relativized. When the object NP is the head of the relative clause, there is a gap in the object position, suggestive of movement. In fact, the standard analysis of relative clauses, clefts, and question formation within generative grammar has treated them as outputs of wh-movement (cf. Chomsky 1977). Sentence (2c) appears to offer some evidence for that analysis. If it is assumed that the object NP is generated in postverbal position, and the string adjacency of the object NP to the verb appears to support that, then the appearance of the object in the initial position within the relativized NP configuration could be construed as a consequence of movement. This will be reviewed further below. At this juncture there is need to resolve the question of whether in double-object constructions both object NPs are accessible to relativization. Consider the following:

(3) a. Anyaní   a-ku-páts-á   njovu   mikánda.
        2-baboons 2SM-pres-give-fv 10-elephants 4-beads
        'The baboons are giving elephants beads.'

   b. Mikándá i-méné   anyaní   á-kú-páts-á   njovu   ndi
       4-beads 4SM-rel 2-baboons 2SM-pres-give-fv 10-elephants be
       y-ó-fíil-a.
       4SM-assoc-red-fv
       'The beads that the baboons are giving the elephants are red.'

   c. ?Njovu   zi-méné anyaní   á-kú-páts-a-á   mikánda
       10-elephants 10SM-rel 2-baboons 2SM-pres-give-fv 4-beads
       zi-má-dy-á   nzímbe.
       10SM-hab-eat-fv 10-sugar canes
       'The elephants that the baboons are giving the beads (to) eat sugar cane.'

The example shows that the two postverbal NPs behave differently with regard to relativization. This will become evident in double-object constructions arising from the morphological processes of causativization and applicativization. The marginal sentence above becomes fully grammatical when the OM that agrees with the relativized object noun is included in the verbal morphology. Consider the following:

   d. Njovu   zi-méné anyaní   á-kú-zí-páts-á   mikánda
       10-elephants 10SM-rel 2-baboons 2SM-pres-10OM-give-fv 4-beads
       zí-ma-dy-á   nzímbe.
       10SM-hab-eat-fv 10-sugar canes
       'The elephants that the baboons are giving the beads (to) eat sugar cane.'

The OM marker is functioning as a resumptive pronoun. The resumptive pronoun strategy is common in Chichewa relative-clause formation. Before reviewing this, one other observation must be made about the relative-clause configuration.

4.4   Tonal marking of the relative clause

In chapter 2 there were comments made about the significance of tone in Chichewa and its involvement in marking certain syntactic configurations. In the analysis of the OM as an incorporated pronominal argument Bresnan and Mchombo (1987) amassed various types of evidence to support that conclusion. The evidence included the behavior of tone within VP configuration. The observation, discussed above (Section 3.3), centered on tonal marking in phrase-final position. It was noted that there were tonal changes that correlated with lengthening of the penultimate syllable. The claim was that the final vowel of the verb bears a high tone when the verb is not in phrase-final position. When it is in phrase-final position, the high tone retracts to a low-toned penultimate syllable, yielding a rising tone. The relevance of tonal patterning to the analysis of the OM was that in the presence of the OM, the tone pattern is characteristic of phrase-final position, providing a phonological cue to the constituency of the verb phrase. The postverbal NP was tonally marked as outside the VP configuration.

The relative construction gives yet another instance of the involvement of tone in marking syntactic configurations. The presence of the relative marker -*méne* also has the phonological effect of marking the verb within the relative construction with a high tone. Comparable observations have been made about relative clauses in Lunda, a language spoken in west-central Africa, particularly in the north-eastern part of Angola, the south-western region of the Democratic Republic of the Congo, and the north-western part of Zambia (Kawasha 1999a, b). When the relative marker -*méne* heads the relative clause, the SM and tense/aspect of the relative clause are marked with high tones. The examples given above illustrate the point. The use of tone to identify the NP configuration licenses the possible omission of the relative marker. In studies of English within the framework of generative grammar, it was noted that the Complementizer (COMP) node could be deleted. This is evident in the sentence below:

(4)   The zebras think (that) the lions will not spot them.

This was extended to relative pronouns, to account for such English constructions as:

(5)   The beads the baboons stole were fake.

In sentence (5), the relative pronoun 'that' or 'which' has been deleted. The rule of COMP Deletion could be extended to cover such cases, demonstrating thereby that the relative pronoun was in COMP position, itself the traditional landing site for wh-movement. However, the rule of COMP Deletion had to be blocked in the case of relativization on the subject because it led to the formation of ungrammatical sentences. The ungrammaticality arose from the apparent change of category of the relative NP configuration into what looked like a main clause. Consider sentences (6a and b) below:

(6) a.   The man who stole the beads was an agent of the baboons.
    b.   *The man stole the beads was an agent of the baboons.

Sentence (6b) is ungrammatical because, as a consequence of deleting the relative pronoun 'who,' the relative NP configuration is construed as a sentence. Allowing free application of syntactic rules, including the rule of COMP Deletion, led to the postulation of filtering devices as an aspect of the machinery of grammatical theory. These would rule out unacceptable outputs. This view was argued for and defended by Chomsky and Lasnik (1977). They proposed free application of transformational rules with the proviso that the output of movement rules would have to satisfy various constraints. Constraints on grammatical theory would shift from rules to representations. The ungrammaticality of sentence (6b) is due in part to garden-path effects.

Tone marking in Chichewa relative constructions obviates the potential derivation of garden-path sentences. Consider sentence (2b), again, repeated below as sentence (7a):

(7) a.   Anyaní   a-méné   á-kú-b-á   mikánda a-ku-dz-éts-á
          2-baboons 2SM-rel 2SM-pres-steal-fv 4-beads 2SM-pres-come-caus-fv
          chisokonezo.
          7-confusion
          'The baboons that are stealing beads are bringing confusion.'

The relative marker -méné can be omitted from the sentence without altering the construal of the configuration:

    b.   Anyaní   á-kú-b-á   mikánda a-ku-dz-éts-á   chisokonezo.
          2-baboons 2SM-pres-steal-fv 4-beads 2SM-pres-come-caus-fv 7-confusion
          'The baboons (that are) stealing beads are bringing confusion.'

The omission of the marker -méné has no consequence on the interpretation of the configuration anyaní á-kú-b-á mikánda 'the baboons that are stealing the beads.' It remains a relative construction because of the tonal marking. This underscores the need for sustained research into interface relations between phonology and syntax.

4.5   The resumptive pronoun strategy

The relative construction in Chichewa could be represented in the following way:

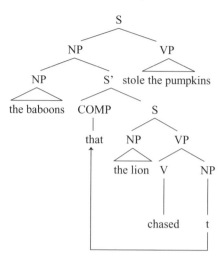

Figure 4.1

The standard treatment of relative clauses as resulting from wh-movement derives from the fact that subcategorization requirements of the verb within the relative clause are not satisfied. The missing argument is construed with the relative pronoun. It functions as the TOPIC element, in anaphoric binding relation with the relativized noun, which is the FOCUS. Naturally, the argument based on violations of subcategorization requirements is undermined when the moved category is referenced by a pronominal within the VP. In Chichewa the OM has been analyzed as an incorporated pronominal argument, generated in its position. The NP in anaphoric agreement with the OM is a discourse-licensed non-argument phrase. Its structural position is not determined by rules of grammar but by discourse structure. Consequently, the relative clause in Chichewa, which routinely exploits the resumptive pronoun strategy through the presence of the OM, could not, conceivably, be handled in terms of wh-movement. It will be maintained that relative-clause formation in Chichewa does not involve movement operations. In this regard, the approach adopted here will be comparable to the one advanced by Biloa for Tuki (Biloa 1990). Note that the non-movement analysis accounts for lack of island violations, especially in the presence of the OM. We will take the OM to be functioning like a pronominal variable bound to the relative operator.

4.6   The relative marker -o

The other strategy for relative-clause formation is that which employs a suffixal -o. The -o is attached to the verb and it is marked for agreement with the relativized noun. Note the following:

(8) a. Mbuzí   zi-méné   mú-kú-zí-fǔn-a   zi-li   pa   chulu.
        10-goats 10SM-rel 2nd pl-pres-10OM-want-fv 10SM-be 16-loc 7-anthill
        'The goats that you want are on the anthill.'

   b.   Mbuzí   mú-kú-zí-fun-ǎ-z-o   zi-li   pa   chulu.
        10-goats 2nd pl-pres-10OM-want-fv-10SM-rel 10SM-be 16-loc 7-anthill
        'The goats that you want are on the anthill.'

This strategy for relative-clause formation has not received widespread attention. A movement account for these relative clauses seems tenuous at best (see Ngonyani 1998b, 1999 for such an approach).

4.7   Question formation

Relative clauses in Chichewa have relevance to question formation. In this language question formation does not have to invoke wh-movement. Question formation is in situ and, where there is apparent movement, it involves a cleft construction (cf. Mchombo and Mtenje 1983). This may be exemplified by the following:

(9) a. Mkángó   u-ku-sáúts-á   yani?
        3-lion   3SM-pres-bother-fv   who
        'Who is the lion bothering?'

   b.   Kodí ndi yani   a-méné   mkángó   ú-kú-(mú)-sáuts-a?
        Q   cop who SM-relpro 3-lion   3SM-pres-(1OM)-bother-fv
        'Who is it that the lion is bothering?'

(10) a. Anyaní   á   mísala   a-ku-chí-pwány-a   chipanda   chá
         2-baboons 2assoc 4-madness 2SM-pres-7OM-smash-fv 7-calabash 7assoc
         kazitápé wá   alenje.
         1a-spy 1assoc 2-hunters
         'The mad baboons are smashing the calabash of the hunters' spy.'

    b.   Kodí anyaní   á   mísala   a-ku-phwány-á   chiyáni?
         Q   2-baboons 2assoc 4-madness 2SM-pres-smash-fv what?
         'What are the mad baboons smashing?'

    c.   Kodí ndi chiyáni chi-méné   anyaní   á   mísala
         Q   cop what   7SM-relpro 2-baboons 2assoc 4-madness
         á-kú-(chí)-phwány-a?
         2SM-(7OM)-smash-fv?
         'What is it that the mad baboons are smashing?'

In (10b), the object is questioned in situ. In (10c), where there appears to be movement, the question formation involves a cleft construction. This, in turn, has a relative construction. The verb can have an incorporated object argument, obviating the need for wh-movement.

The cleft construction is comparable to that in English. It involves the copula *ndi* or the negative copula *sí* that marks the FOCUS element, then followed by the relative marker *-méné*, appropriately marked for agreement with the focused element. The relative marker heads a relative clause. Consider the following:

(11) a.   Ndi anyaní   á   mísála   a-méné á-kú-phwány-á
        cop 2-baboons 2SM-assoc 4-madness 2SM-rel 2SM-pres-smash-fv
        chipanda.
        7-calabash
        'It's the mad baboons that are smashing the calabash.'

    b.   Sí   chikho chi-méné anyaní   á   mísala
        neg-cop 7-gourd 7SM-rel 2-baboons 2SM-assoc 4-madness
        á-kú-phwăny-a.
        2SM-pres-smash-fv
        'It's not a gourd that the mad baboons are smashing.'

The OM can, of course, appear in the verbal morphology of the verb in the relative clause. In question formation, when the focused element is the object NP, it is questioned in situ, more so when the OM is absent. On the other hand, in the presence of the OM the agreeing NP cannot be questioned in situ. The cleft construction is invoked in that case. In some respects, this is because the agreeing object already has a discourse function of TOPIC. Questioning it in situ would make it acquire an additional discourse function of FOCUS. It seems that there is a constraint on an element having different functions at the same level of clause structure. The assignment of both TOPIC and FOCUS to the same element at the same level of clause structure leads to functional clash, as noted by Bresnan and Mchombo (1987). In the cleft construction, the FOC is sister to the clause that has the relative marker *-méné*, which functions as the TOP element. The derivation of clefts thus need not involve movement given that the FOC element is not an argument of the verb. It is in anaphoric binding relation with the incorporated pronominal argument functioning as a resumptive pronoun. The FOC element is the one replaced by the wh-word *chiyáni* 'what' in questions that have the semblance of movement. The FOC element is linked to the TOP marker *-méné* which is functionally identified by the missing argument in the relative clause or is linked anaphorically to the resumptive OM pronominal argument.

4.8   More on subject marker and object marker

In their analysis of the S(ubject) M(arker) and O(bject) M(arker) in Chichewa, Bresnan and Mchombo argued that the OM is an incorporated pronominal argument not a non-referential marker of grammatical agreement. The evidence from both Chichewa and other Bantu languages supports the analysis (cf. Chimbutane 2002; Demuth and Johnson 1989; Dlayedwa 2002; Matambirofa 2002; Omar 1990; Rubanza 1988; Sabimana 1986; Thwala 1995). The analysis has not, however, extended easily to the status of the SM. Bresnan and Mchombo claimed that

> the SM on our analysis is indeed such a marker; it also has a referential use, under appropriate conditions, as an incorporated pronoun. This implies that all simple SuV [Subject–Verb – SM] sentences are functionally ambiguous; the apparent subject NP could either be a true subject with which the verb shows grammatical agreement . . . , or it could be a topic NP related by anaphoric agreement to the subject pronominal in the verb . . .   (Bresnan and Mchombo 1987: 755)

The SM is thus functionally ambiguous. It is used as a marker of grammatical agreement when it agrees with a nominal that has the function of Subject and, when it is used for anaphoric binding, its antecedent within the sentence has the TOP function. The prediction is that such functional ambiguity should provide explanation for syntactic differences between the SM and OM and between grammatical and anaphoric agreement. Recent work on agreement and dislocation in Kinande, another Bantu language, bears on the differences between the SM and OM (cf. Baker 2003). In Chichewa one construction where the two markers might behave differently is question construction. The SM, it has been indicated, is obligatory. Consider the construction involving a questioned subject NP:

(12) a. Anyaní   á   mísala   a-ku-phwány-á   maûngu.
       2-baboons 2assoc 4-madness 2SM-pres-smash-fv 6-pumpkins
       'The mad baboons are smashing pumpkins.'

   b. Kodí ndǎni a-ku-phwány-á   maûngu?
      Q   who   1SM-pres-smash-fv 6-pumpkins
      'Who is smashing pumpkins?'

   c. Kodí ndǎni á-kú-phwány-á   maûngu?
      Q   who   1SM-pres-smash-fv 6-pumpkins
      'Who is smashing pumpkins?'

The question word *ndǎni* means 'who.' It seems to derive from *ndi+yani*, a compounding of the copula *ndi* with the basic question word *yani*. The question word *chiyani* 'what' has the class marker for class 7, the class that contains the word *chinthu* 'thing.' The class marker is attached to *yani* to derive 'what.' *Ndǎni*, on the other hand, originated as 'it is who.' Although the word is used to mean 'who,' its connection to the cleft constructions remains evident.

Observe that when the subject NP is the focused element, there are two strategies for the question construction. The strategy given in (12b) is a genuine in situ question formation. This is not merely signaled by the position of the question word *ndăni*, but also by the tone marking on the verb. For some speakers of Chichewa, and in some registers, the question word replaces the focused NP and the expression retains the tone pattern characteristic of a sentence. The verb in the sentence has the SM and the rest of the required elements. Such a construction was seen to be impossible with the OM. The NP agreeing with the OM cannot be questioned within the same clause as the OM, something that the SM seems to tolerate, indicating its status as a grammatical agreement marker.

On the other hand, it also manifests its status as an incorporated pronoun by allowing the use of the cleft construction in question formation. This is shown in (12c). The clue there is in the tone pattern of the verb. Although the TOP element *-méné* is missing, and possible omission of this element has been commented upon already, the tone marking signals the presence of a relative construction. This means that the question is, literally, of the form, 'it is who that is smashing pumpkins.' The difference in question formation strategy between the SM and OM lends further credence to the analysis of the SM as functionally ambiguous between marker of grammatical agreement and an incorporated pronoun. There is also another area where the SM and OM might have different consequences. This is in the formation of constructions where the constituents of the NPs agreeing with the SM and OM are discontinuous. Discontinuity of the constituents of the NPs is intimately connected to the head marking of the verb with the SM and OM. This seems to bear further proof of the status of these elements as pronominal arguments. We turn to the issue immediately.

4.9   Discontinuous noun phrases in Chichewa

Noun phrases are associated with a number of properties. For instance, NPs may contain an arbitrary number of subconstituents that result from recursion in phrase structure. This happens, for instance, when the NP contains a preposi-tional phrase that, in turn, contains another NP. Further, NPs typically occur with an identifiable head noun. Constituent integrity of the NP is shown by occurrence of NPs in "derived" environments, such as topicalization, cleft, etc. (cf. Kathol and Rhodes 2000, for relevant observations). In general, the possibility for "splitting" nominal constituents apart is extremely restricted. Consider the following data:

(13) a. Njúchí   izi   zi-ná-lúm-á   álenje   awa   ópúsa.
         10-bees 10proxdem 10SM-pst-bite-fv   2-hunters   2proxdem   2SM-foolish
         'These bees bit these foolish hunters.'

   b. Mikángó i-tátu   i-ná-gúmúl-á   makólá   ónse a-náyi.
       4-lions   4SM-three 4SM-pst-pull down-fv 6-corrals all   6SM-four
       'Three lions pulled down all the four corrals.'

In these examples the nominal phrases have internal constituents. The integrity of the NPs can be shown by their occurrence in such derived environments as passive, in (14a) below, and cleft in (14b):

(14) a. Álenje   awa   ópúsa   a-ná-lúm-ídw-á   ndí njúchí
         2-hunters 2proxdem 2SM-foolish 2SM-pst-bite-pass-fv by 10-bees
         izi.
         10proxdem
         'These foolish hunters were bitten by these bees.'

   b.   Ndi makólá   ónse a-náyi   a-méné   mikángó   i-tátu
         Cop 6-corrals all 6SM-four 6SM-relpro 4-lions   4SM-three
         í-ná-gúmŭl-a.
         4SM-pst-pull down-fv
         'It was all the four corrals that the three lions pulled down.'

In the absence of the OM not only must the object NP remain in postverbal position and maintain string adjacency with the verb, but its internal constituency cannot be disrupted. The ungrammaticality of sentences in (15) illustrates that.

(15) a. *Awa   njúchí izi   zi-ná-lúmá   **alenje**   **ópúsa**.
         2proxdem 10-bees 10proxdem 10SM-pst-bite 2-hunters foolish

   b.   *Awa   ópúsa njúchí izi   zi-ná-lúmá   **alenje**.
         2proxdem foolish 10-bees 10proxdem 10SM-pst-bite 2-hunters

It has already been indicated that within a noun phrase in Chichewa, nominal modifiers are marked for agreement with the head noun. Thus, in the nominal expressions appearing in the sentences above, the proximal demonstrative 'these' is conveyed by *izi* in the NP *njúchí izi* 'these bees' and *awa* in the NP *alenje awa ópúsa* 'these foolish hunters.' Even the modifier *ópúsa* 'foolish' is marked for agreement with *alenje* 'hunters.' Were it to modify *njúchí* to yield 'foolish bees,' the expression would have been *njúchí zópúsa*. The ungrammaticality of the sentences above is directly traceable to the discontinuity of the subconstituents of the object NP. However, when the OM is included in the verbal morphology the results are radically different. Consider the sentences in (16) below, which all have the same cognitive meaning:

(16) a. Njúchí izi   zi-ná-**wá**-lúm-á   álenje   awa
         10-bees 10proxdem 10SM-pst-2OM-bite-fv 2-hunters 2proxdem
         ópúsa.
         2SM-foolish

   b.   **Awa**   njúchí izi   zi-ná-**wá**-lúm-a   **alenje**
         2-proxdem 10-bees 10proxdem 10SM-pst-2OM-bite-fv 2-hunters
         ópúsa.
         2SM-foolish

c. **Alenje** zi-ná-**wá**-lúm-a   njúchí izi   **awa**
    2-hunters 10SM-pst-2OM-bite-fv 10-bees 10-proxdem 2-proxdem
    ópúsa.
    2SM-foolish

d. Izi   **awa**   **ópúsa**   zi-ná-**wá**-lúm-a   **alenje**
    10-proxdem 2proxdem 2SM-foolish 10SM-pst-2OM-bite-fv 2-hunters
    njúchi.
    10-bees
    'These bees bit these foolish hunters.'

In (16a), the OM has been introduced. Its presence does not only make for free word order of the NPs and the verb, as noted in the previous chapters but, in addition, the internal constituents of the NPs can also be discontinuous. This applies to the constituents of both NPs, as shown by the data. That is, the NP functioning as the subject can also have its constituents be discontinuous.

The data suggest that the possibility of discontinuity of the subconstituents of the NPs is apparently induced by the presence of the pronominal arguments. Free word order and the possibility of syntactically discontinuous constituents constitute some of the defining characteristics of non-configurationality. According to Hale (1983) and, for further and more detailed discussion, Speas (1990) as well as Austin and Bresnan (1996), the hallmarks of non-configurationality in natural language include the following:

(i)   free word order
(ii)   syntactically discontinuous expressions
(iii)   null anaphora.

The data presented appear to suggest that Chichewa has the basic properties of non-configurational languages. It could thus be classified as non-configurational despite the traditional view that Bantu languages are configurational (cf. Morimoto 2002). Whatever the classification of Bantu languages in general, and Chichewa in particular, may be along the configurationality parameter, certain questions arise concerning the data. These include the following:

(i)   What is the nature of the connection between head marking and discontinuous constituents?
(ii)   Does head marking induce discontinuity of the NPs in every case or are there NPs whose integrity cannot be violated even under head marking?
(iii)   If there are such NPs, what explains their resistance to the splitting of their constituents?

4.10   Head marking and discontinuous constituents

Marking the verb head with the pronominal arguments satisfies the argument-structure requirements of the verb. The agreeing NPs are, in all relevant respects, like adjuncts. In this regard, the effects of head marking in Chichewa are comparable to pronominal argument marking in Australian languages. They have the net effect that the pronominal arguments bear the syntactic functions of subject and object. They also bear thematic roles and, as evidenced in the restricted domain of personal pronouns, manifest changes associated with case marking. The SM and OM are pronominal arguments and the nominal expressions are generated in non-argument, adjunct positions. That the nominal expression linked to the OM has the discourse function of TOPIC is, by now, established from a number of languages. There are still questions surrounding the status of the SM and the nominal expression that agrees with it. These do not undermine the status of the SM as a pronominal argument and, with regard to the creation of discontinuous constituents, the SM, just like the OM, is implicated in that. The SM can, thus, be taken to function as the SUBJ, an analysis advocated by Demuth and Johnson for the Bantu language of Setawana (Demuth and Johnson 1989). Part of the evidence for regarding the SM as a pronominal argument bearing the SUBJ function derives from its ability to, *inter alia*, be the antecedent for the reflexive.

In many Bantu languages the reflexive morpheme is invariant, and appears in the position of the OM. Consider the following Chichewa sentence:

(17) a.   Mikángó í-ma-dzi-kând-a.
           4-lions   4SM-hab-reflex-scratch-fv
           'Lions scratch themselves.'

   b.   Mikángó i-ku-úz-á   anyáni   kutí sí-í-ku-fún-á   kutí
        4-lions   4SM-pres-tell-fv 2-baboons that neg-4SM-pres-want that
        njovu   zi-dzíw-é   kutí í-ma-dzi-kǎnd-a.
        10-elephants 10SM-know-subjun that 4SM-hab-reflex-scratch-fv
        'The lions are telling the baboons that they don't want the elephants to know
        that they (lions) scratch themselves.'

In these examples, the reflexive is bound to the nominal *mikángo* 'lions,' in (17a), constrained by appropriate structural conditions of being bound within the minimal clause in which it is contained. In (17b) the reflexive still has the nominal *mikángo* 'lions' as its antecedent. However, the antecedent is not within the same simple clause but a few clauses higher. The binding is facilitated by the reflexive being bound within its local domain by the SM, a pronominal argument that is functioning as the SUBJ, also satisfying the relevant command relation. The SM is in anaphoric relation with the nominal *mikángo* 'lions.'

Granting that the SM is a pronominal argument, and that the presence of the SM and OM in the verbal morphology effectively satisfies the requirements of lexical structure, what bearing does that have on discontinuity of the constituents of the nominal adjuncts? A suggestion advanced by Jelinek (1984) is that the constituents of the nominal expression can themselves be regarded as nominals, and that they are referentially linked to the pronominal arguments. This would be consistent with standard assumptions about anaphoric relations, which require that a pronominal be free within an appropriately defined local domain. It also gets support from the fact that the nominal modifiers, such as the demonstrative *awa* '2-these' or *izi* '10-these' could be used independently of the accompanying head nouns; the same with the adnominal *ópúsa* '2-foolish.' Thus, the sentences below are grammatical:

(18) a.   Awa   zi-na-wá-lúm-a   izi.
          2-these 10SM-pst-2OM-bite-fv 10-these
          'These (hunters), they bit them, these (bees).'
          lit. 'These (bees) bit them, these (hunters).'

    b.   Ópúsa   zi-na-wá-lúm-a   izi.
          2-foolish 10SM-pst-2OM-bite-fv 10-these
          'These (bees) bit them, the foolish ones.'

The examples above show that antecedents in anaphoric relation with the pronominal arguments can be demonstratives or other adnominals, with which they agree in φ-features.

Such an analysis of the relation between head marking and discontinuity of the constituents of the nominal adjuncts has some weaknesses. For a start, it is consistent with a structure where several nominal expressions could be present, agreeing in φ-features with the pronominal arguments, but not comprising a constituent. This is exemplified by the following:

(19)   *Alenje   njúchí zi-na-wá–lúm-a   asodzi.
        2-hunters 10-bee 10SM-pst-2OM-bite-fv 2-fishermen
        '*The hunters the bees bit them the fishermen.'

The two nominals 'hunters' and 'fishermen' agree with the OM, but the sentence is ungrammatical. They do not form a constituent, leading to violation of, *inter alia*, the theta-criterion or projection principle within the theory of Principles and Parameters, or the Coherence Condition within the theory of Lexical Functional Grammar, or their equivalents in other theories. What is required is the deployment of some mechanism to capture the fact that the expressions linked to the pronominal arguments constitute a constituent at some level of representation. Within the Principles and Parameters Theory, the natural procedure is to derive the overt structure from a basic underlying representation where the integrity of the nominal expression is preserved. The overt structure would result from the application of the rule-schema Move-α, as noted by Pollock; it is the one fundamental claim of transformational grammar that "sentences can be paired with a number of different syntactic representations" (Pollock 1989: 378).

Such an approach is, essentially, the one advocated by Matthewson and Reinholtz (1996), Russell and Reinholtz (1996), and Reinholtz (1999) in studies of Swampy Cree. Reinholtz takes issue with the approach advocated by Jelinek of analyzing the discontinuous constituents of the NP as separate noun phrases that are referentially linked to the same pronominal argument. Part of the argument rests on the behavior of obliques in Swampy Cree. In that language, phrases expressing oblique arguments such as source, goal, and instrument are not included in the pronominal argument hypothesis (see also Austin and Bresnan, cited above). As such, if referential linking to the pronominal argument were necessary to the formation of discontinuous constituents, then oblique arguments, not referentially linked to incorporated arguments, would be predicted to resist discontinuity. However, "[T]he behavior of oblique phrases contradicts this prediction, suggesting that the formation of discontinuous constituents is determined by factors independent of referential linking" (Reinholtz 1999: 215). In brief, oblique arguments in Swampy Cree can be discontinuous. Other considerations based on the distribution of nominal quantifiers and adverbial phrases appear to be consistent with the referential linking analysis, so no further comment will be made about them.

Russell and Reinholtz (1996) and Reinholtz (1999), building on that earlier work, propose to deal with discontinuous constituents in the traditional fashion of invoking movement. The claim is that in Swampy Cree the displaced modifier has the discourse function of FOCUS. This suggests that "discontinuous NPs may thus be characterized as the output of a Focus mechanism which picks out the nominal modifier in a larger NP and places it in a preverbal Focus position, where it appears separately from the noun it qualifies" (Reinholtz 1999: 208). Movement to FOCUS position has generally been identified with wh-movement. It should, therefore, be the case that discontinuous constituents must be a result of wh-movement. Besides, evidence from Swampy Cree lends further credence to such an analysis in that "both movement types show the ability to span several clauses, a limited application in relative clauses or embedded questions, and an inability to move any material out of adverbial constituents" (Reinholtz 1999: 218).

There are several problems with this analysis. Data from Chichewa support the prediction about obliques not submitting to discontinuity, despite contrary evidence from Swampy Cree. For instance, an instrumental phrase in a non-applicative construction cannot be discontinuous. This is illustrated below:

(20) a. Mikángó yókálamba i-ná-zí-gúmúl-a   ndí   makású awa
         4-lions   4SM-aged   4SM-pst-10OM-demolish-fv with   6-hoes 6-these
         óbúntha   nkhókwe.
         6SM-blunt 10-granaries
         'The aged lions pulled down the granaries with these blunt hoes.'

      b. *Awa   búntha   mikángó yókálamba i-na-zí-gúmúl-a   ndí
          6-these 6SM-blunt 4-lions   4SM-aged   SM-pst-10OM-demolish-fv with
          mákásu nkhókwe.
          6-hoes 10-granaries

In addition to that, in an applicative construction, such as when the applicative introduces a beneficiary, only the applied object has the properties associated with the primary object. Chichewa, like Kiswahili, is an asymmetric language (cf. Alsina and Mchombo 1993; Bresnan and Moshi 1990; Ngonyani 1998a). In such constructions only the applied object, the benefactive, agrees with the OM. Below is an example:

(21) a. Anyání   a-na-í-gúl-íl-á   makású awa   óbúntha
         2-baboons 2SM-pst-4OM-buy-appl-fv 6-hoes 6-these 6SM-blunt
         mikángó yókálamba.
         4-lions   4SM-aged
         'The baboons bought (for) the lions these blunt hoes.'

The noun phrase expressing the theme *makású awa óbúntha* 'these blunt hoes' cannot be in anaphoric relation with the incorporated pronominal object. Only the applied object *mikángó yókálamba* 'aged lions,' marking the benefactive, can have its features duplicated by the OM. Note that the benefactive can indeed be discontinuous. The theme, on the other hand, either must not be discontinuous, as shown in (21c) below, or can tolerate discontinuity only when the head noun is fronted for FOCUS, with the modifiers remaining in postverbal position in apposition to the head noun. This is shown in (21d) below.

Besides, in the ordering relation, the theme must precede the benefactive, indicating the benefactive's role as an adjunct, outside the nuclear clause:

      b. Yókálamba anyání   a-na-í-gúl-íl-á   makású awa
          4SM-aged   2-baboons 2SM-pst-4OM-buy-appl-fv 6-hoes 6-these
          óbúntha   mikángo.
          6SM-blunt 4-lions
          'The baboons bought the aged lions these blunt hoes.'

      c. *Awa   óbúntha   anyání   a-na-í-gúl-íl-a   makású
          6-these 6SM-blunt 2-baboons 2SM-pst-4OM-buy-appl-fv 6-hoes
          mikángó yókálamba.
          4-lions   4SM-aged

> d. Makású anyání a-na-í-gúl-íl-á awa óbúntha
> 6-hoes 2-baboons 2SM-pst-4OM-buy-appl-fv 6-these 6SM-blunt
> mikángo yókálamba.
> 4-lions 4SM-aged
> 'As for hoes, the baboons bought the aged lions these blunt ones.'

Similar considerations apply to the possessor-raising construction. Chichewa has constructions related by the applicative in the following manner:

> (22) a. Mkángó u-ku-dy-á maúngú a á amalinyêlo.
> 3-lion 3SM-pres-eat-fv 6-pumpkins 6SM-assoc 2-sailors
> 'The lion is eating the sailors' pumpkins.'
>
> b. Mkángó u-ku-dy-él-á amalinyéló maûngu.
> 3-lion 3SM-pres-eat-appl-fv 2-sailors 6-pumpkins
> 'The lion is eating the sailors' pumpkins.'

In (22a) the possessor of the pumpkins *amalinyêlo* 'sailors' in the genitive construction *maúngú á amalinyêlo* 'pumpkins of the sailors' has been "raised" and functions as the object of the applicative construction. The construction also has a malefactive reading, that is, that the lion is eating the pumpkins against the wishes of the sailors (for discussion of malefactive applicatives, see chapter 5). The status of *amalinyêlo* 'sailors' as the object is indicated in part by its accessibility to passivization, as well as by its ability to control object marking, as shown in (22c and d) below:

> c. Amalinyéló a-ku-dy-él-édw-á maûngu ndí mkángo.
> 2-sailors 2SM-pres-eat-appl-pass-fv 6-pumpkins by 3-lion
> 'The sailors are having (their) pumpkins eaten for them by the lion.'
>
> d. Mkángó u-ku-**wá**-dy-él-á maûngu **amalinyêlo**.
> 3-lion 3SM-pres-2OM-eat-appl-fv 6-pumpkins 2-sailor.
> 'The lion is eating the pumpkins for them (the sailors).'

With respect to discountinuity, only the raised possessor, *amalinyêlo*, cross-referenced by the OM, can be discontinuous. This is illustrated by the following:

> e. Mkángó u-ku-**wá**-dy-él-á *maúngú áákûlu* **amalinyéló**
> 3-lion 3SM-pres-2OM-eat-appl-fv 6-pumpkins 6SM-big 2-sailors
> **ó-gúnata**.
> 2assoc-foolish
> 'The lion is eating for the foolish sailors (their) big pumpkins.'

Observe that the NP *maúngú áákûlu* 'big pumpkins' cannot be discontinuous, as shown below:

> f. * *áákûlu* mkángó u-ku-**wá**-dy-él-á *maûngu* **amalinyéló ógúnata**

On the other hand, *amalinyéló ó-gúnata* 'foolish sailors,' the raised possessor, in anaphoric relation with the OM, can be discontinuous:

g. **ógúnata**   mkángó u-ku-**wá**-dy-él-á   *maúngú   áákûlu*
    2assoc-foolish 3-lion   3SM-pres-2OM-eat-appl-fv 6-pumpkins 6SM-big
    amalinyêlo.
    2-sailors
    'The lion is eating for the foolish sailors (their) big pumpkins.'

Jelinek's prediction is, thus, not wide of the mark in Chichewa. Another problem, also noted by the authors, is that a movement analysis of discontinuous constituents increases the range of movement rules, increasing the power of the rule schema, with corresponding reduction of constraints on the theory of grammar. This is because the movement is of constituents out of nominal adjuncts, to adjunct positions. The movement can neither be assimilated to wh-movement despite claims to that effect (cf. Reinholtz 1999), nor to NP movement or head (X^o)-movement. A general restriction on movement, formulated by Huang (1982), called the Condition on Extraction Domain (CED), restricts movement to elements that are in domains of proper government. Such domains include being structural objects of one of a small class of transitive heads, such as transitive verb or preposition, or one of the functional categories of Tense or Agreement. Adjuncts do not serve as proper governors. They are thus not expected to allow extraction under the CED.

Noting the problems that discontinuous constituents pose for the theory of grammar adopted in their work, Russell and Reinholtz, and Reinholtz especially, conclude that there is need to review the range of allowable movement operations in natural language and the status of CED. The conclusion arrived at is that there are grounds to maintain that "proper government does not determine whether constituents permit extraction, at least in the case of a pronominal argument language such as Cree" (Reinholtz 1999: 222).

The idea of allowing extraction out of adjuncts, in violation of the CED, has been suggested for the Bantu language Tuki, spoken in Cameroon. Biloa observed that movement operations in Tuki can violate island constraints in that "Tuki allows extraction from relative clauses, embedded questions . . . , and adjuncts" (Biloa 1990: 221).

The problems posed by discontinuous constituents for grammatical theory are real. However, the suggestion of weakening the grammar through a proliferation of varieties of movement operations is unsatisfactory. In our discussion of question formation, clefts, and relative clauses, we have maintained the view that the derivation of these constructions does not and need not invoke movement operations, specifically wh-movement. This is an extension of a view that even in the formation of passive, causative, and applicative constructions, there is no need to invoke movement of categories. This view is consonant or consistent with the claims of the theory of Lexical Functional Grammar (LFG). According to this theory natural language is decomposable into parallel information structures, related non-derivationally (without movement) but, rather, through linking procedures or constraint satisfaction. Although the theory together with its machinery will not be discussed here, it will be implicit in the analyses. There are studies available that deal with the theoretical aspects of LFG (for relevant discussion of the theory see Bodomo 1997; Bresnan 2001; Dalrymple 2001; Falk 2001; King 1995; Horrocks 1987; Lee 2001; Nordlinger 1998).

Within the theory informing this study, there is factorization of informational structures into parallel representations, with mechanisms for linking the different informational capsules in non-derivational fashion. Discourse structure is represented separately from argument structure and functional structure, and the relation between the parallel levels of representation is non-derivational. Adopting the tenets of such a theory, there is no need to invoke, let alone extend the range of, movement rules. Such rules do not exist. We will adopt a version of a theory of grammar in which there is such a separation of lexical structure, syntactic structure, and discourse structure, into distinct parallel representations, with principled linkages among them.

Adopting such a framework leads to the claim that the relation between the pronominal argument and the discontinuous nominal adjuncts could be handled in terms of referential linking or anaphoric binding. The discontinuity of the constituents of the nominal adjuncts is not a result of movement; rather, it has to do with the mapping of an inner structure of grammatical representation to its outer or overt organization.

4.11   Limits of discontinuity

There are restrictions on the discontinuity of the constituents of nominal adjuncts in anaphoric relation with the pronominal arguments. Among the configurations that appear to resist discontinuity of their constituents are relative clauses. Consider the following:

(23)   Mkángó u-méné   ú-ma-sáká   mbûzi   ú-ma-wa-saútsa
        3-lion   3SM-relpro 3SM-hab-hunt 10SM-goats 3SM-hab-2OM-bother
        alenje   a-méné   á-ma-gwetsá   mitêngo.
        2-hunters 2SM-relpro 2SM-hab-fell 4-trees
        'The lion which hunts goats bothers the hunters who fell trees.'

The formation of relative clauses in Chichewa has been discussed above. The use of the OM as a resumptive pronoun, obviating the need for assimilating relative clauses to the effects of wh-movement has been reviewed. According to Biloa "[I]n Tuki headed relative clauses, the head of the relative clause can be associated either with a resumptive pronoun or a variable" (Biloa 1990: 216). A resumptive pronoun is characterized as a pronoun which appears in wh-movement constructions and which is directly bound by an operator in such constructions. In Tuki, the resumptive pronoun can be either overt or phonologically null. The presence of the resumptive pronouns makes for apparent island violations. Returning to Chichewa, consider the following, in which we will be reminded of the role that tone plays in relative constructions:

(24) a.   Mkángó u-ku-sáká   mbûzi.
           3-lion   3SM-pres-hunt 10-goats
           'The lion is hunting goats.'

     b.   Mkángó u-méné   ú-kú-sáká   mbûzi
           3-lion   3SM-relpro 3SM-pres-hunt 10-goats
           'The lion which is hunting goats'

The tone patterns on the verb *ukusáka* 'it is hunting' are different, correlating with whether the expression is a main clause or a relative NP configuration. Sentence (24c) below illustrates the omission of the relative marker -*méné*, with tone providing the cue for the syntactic configuration:

     c.   Mkángó ú-kú-sáká   mbûzi
           3-lion   3SM-pres-hunt 10-goats
           'The lion which is hunting goats'

Returning to sentence (23) above, the verb *sautsa* 'bother, trouble' is marked with the SM for class 3 *u* agreeing with *mkángó* 'lion' and the OM *wa*, agreeing with *alenje* 'hunters.' While the order of the nominal expressions *mkángó u-méné ú-ma-sáká mbûzi* 'the lion which hunts goats' and *alenje a-méné á-ma-gwétsá mitêngo* 'the hunters who fell the trees' is free, the constituents of those nominal expressions cannot be discontinuous. The following sentence is, at best, questionable:

(25)   ?**alenje**   *mkángó* ú-ma-**wa**-saútsa   **a-méné**   **á-ma-gwetsá**
        2-hunters 3-lion   3SM-hab-2OM-bother 2SM-relpro 2SM-hab-fell
        miténgo *u-méné*   *ú-ma-saká*   *mbúzi.*
        4-trees   3SM-relpro 3SM-hab-hunt 10-goats
        'The hunters the lion bothers them, who fell trees, that hunts goats.'

The nominal expressions are relativized NPs. The possibility of extraposing the relative clause, possible in Chichewa, does not completely rescue the sentence from ungrammaticality. The object NPs within those relative clauses cannot be moved out largely because the verbal head is itself not marked with the OM. Now consider the following where the verbal heads within the relative clauses are marked with resumptive OMs:

(26)   Mkángo u-méné   ú-ma-**zi**-saka   **mbûzi** ú-ma-*wa*-sautsa
       3-lion   2SM-relpro 3SM-hab-hunt 10-goats 3SM-hab-2OM-bother
       alenje   a-méné   a-ma-<u>i</u>-gwetsa <u>miténgo</u>.
       2-hunters 3SM-relpro 2SM-hab-fell   4-trees
       'The lion which hunts the goats bothers the hunters that fell the trees.'

This sentence does not allow for the range of possible word orders that are normally associated with head marking in Chichewa. The nominal adjuncts, which contain relative clauses, cannot be scrambled despite the presence of the resumptive pronouns within them. Thus, the following sentences are ungrammatical:

(27) a.   *Mkángo **mbûzi**   *alenje*   <u>miténgo</u> ú-ma-*wa*-sautsa
          3-lion   10-goats 2-hunters 4-trees   3SM-hab-2OM-bother
          u-méné   u-ma-**zi**-saka a-méné   a-ma-<u>i</u>-gwetsa
          3SM-relpro SM-hab-hunt 2SM-relpro 2SM-hab-fell

     b.   ***Mbûzi**   mkángo u-méné   ú-ma-**zi**-saka <u>miténgo</u>
          10-goats 3-lion   3SM-relpro SM-hab-hunt 4-trees
          alenje   a-méné   a-ma-<u>i</u>-gwetsa *ú*-ma-*wa*-sautsa
          2-hunters 2SM-relpro 2SM-hab-fell   3SM-hab-2OM-bother

The problem here probably rests on the multiplicity of nominal expressions with similar discourse functions, making for processing or information-structuring difficulties. Still, in general, when the nominal expressions have relative clauses, discontinuity among the constituents is more difficult. This could be reduced to island effects, independent of movement despite the tradition of subsuming relativization under wh-movement (Chomsky 1977; Ngonyani 1996, 1998b). Relative-clause formation in Chichewa demonstrates the absence of motivation for analysis in movement terms. Biloa maintains a similar stance with regard to relative-clause formation in Tuki, suggesting that wh- is generated in COMP. I will review the situation for Chichewa.

4.12   Genitive constructions

Relative constructions provide one instance where discontinuity is difficult. Another construction that tolerates discontinuity of the constituents of the nominal adjunct only within limits is the genitive construction. This is a nominal phrase in which the complement to the head noun is introduced by the associative marker *á* 'of'. This is exemplified by the following:

(28)   chipanda   chá   kazitápe
        7-calabash 7SM-assoc 1a-spy
        'The spy's calabash'
        (lit. 'calabash of spy')

Now consider sentence (29) below:

(29)   Anyaní   á   mísala   a-ku-chí-phwány-a   chipanda   chá
        2-baboons 2assoc   4-madness   2SM-pres-7OM-smash-fv 7-calabash 7assoc
        kazitápé wá   alenje.
        1a-spy   1assoc   2-hunters
        'The mad baboons are smashing the calabash of the hunters' spy.'

In this, the main verb *phwanya* 'smash' has the pronominal arguments agreeing
with the nominal adjuncts. Reordering the nominal expressions does not pose any
problems. However, discontinuity of the constituents of the nominal expressions
is only tolerable within limits. Consider the following:

(30) a.   Chá   kazitápé wá   alenje   anyaní   á   mísala
          7assoc   1a-spy   1assoc   2-hunters 2-baboon 2assoc   4-madness
          a-ku-chí-phwány-a   chipanda.
          2SM-pres-7OM-smash-fv   7-calabash

     b.   *Wá   alenje   anyaní   á   mísala   a-ku-chí-phwány-a
          1assoc   2-hunters 2-baboon 2assoc   4-madness   2SM-pres-7OM-smash-fv
          chipanda   chá   kazitápe.
          7-calabash 7assoc   1a-spy

Sentence (30b) is ungrammatical whereas (30a) is grammatical. The obvious
difference in these is that in the grammatical sentence, the discontinuous constituents consist of the complement of the noun whose φ-features agree with those
of the OM, and the head noun itself. In the case of the ungrammatical sentence,
the discontinuous constituents consist of a complement of a noun that is itself
a complement of a higher noun. How can this be accounted for? One approach
would be to subsume this to constraints on movement. One could invoke something along the lines of the A-over-A constraint or, possibly, a modified version of
the Left Branch Condition of Ross (1967). This still remains inconsistent with the
requirements on movement imposed by the CED.

An alternative analysis would be one along the lines of the referential linking proposal of Jelinek. If the discontinuous constituents are treated as nominal
expressions referentially linked to the incorporated pronominal argument, then the
ungrammaticality of (30b) arises from the clash in the φ-features of *wá alenje* 'of
the hunters' with those of the OM. In a sense, the expression *wá alenje* 'of the
hunters' cannot be linked to the pronominal argument. The problem is actually
more involved than that. It is not simply the clash in φ-features between the OM

and the components of the nominal adjunct. The degree of embedding is relevant. The discontinuous constituents must comprise the head noun and the whole unit headed by the associative marker that introduces the complement and is in agreement with it. The restriction is on discontinuity of the constituents of a more embedded complement, that is, a complement of a genitive NP that is itself complement to a head of a complement of the higher head. Agreement of φ-features is not sufficient to restore grammaticality. Consider sentence (31), in which the φ-features of the two phrases headed by the associative marker agree with those of the OM:

(31)   Anyaní   á   mísala   a-ku-chí-phwány-a   chipanda   chá
        2-baboons 2assoc 4-madness 2SM-pres-7OM-smash-fv   7-calabash 7assoc
        chiphadzúwá   chá   alenje.
        7-beauty queen 7SM-assoc   2-hunters
        'The mad baboons are smashing the calabash of the hunters' beauty queen.'

In this, the agreement features of the OM are similar to those of both *chipanda* 'calabash' and *chiphadzúwa* 'beauty queen.' Discontinuity of *chipanda* with the rest of the phrase is possible. But when the discontinuity is that of the complement of *chiphadzúwa* with the rest of the phrase, the results remain ungrammatical. This, in spite of lack of clash in agreement features between *chá alenje* 'of the hunters' and the OM. This is shown in (32) below:

(32)   *Chá   alenje   anyaní   á   mísala
        1assoc 2-hunters   2-baboons 2assoc 4-madness
        a-ku-chí-phwány-a   chipanda   chá   chiphadzúwa
        2SM-pres-7OM-smash-fv   7-calabash 7SM-assoc   7-beauty queen

Obviously the level of embedding is relevant in this case. It is an open question as to whether the same applies to the relative clauses. Either way, in their involvement with the occurrence of discontinuous constituents, the SM and the OM function comparably. This lends credence to their analysis as incorporated pronominal arguments. Their presence is relevant to the discussion of clause structure in Chichewa.

4.13   Conclusion

In this chapter we have focused further on clause structure. Attention was focused on nominal complementation, with emphasis on relative clauses and their involvement in clefts and in question formation. The role of the SM and OM in these constructions was reviewed. It was shown that while the OM is definitely a pronominal argument, the SM remains functionally ambiguous. It functions as a marker of agreement with the subject NP in some cases, and as a pronominal argument in others. In this latter capacity it is comparable to the OM in inducing discontinuity of the constituents of the nominal adjuncts that they agree with. The possibility of discontinuity of the constituents of the nominal adjuncts, together with head marking of the pronominal arguments, gives Chichewa, and possibly other Bantu languages, the property of (partial) non-configurationality. In the next chapter attention will shift from clause structure to argument structure.

5

Argument structure and verb-stem morphology

5.1   Introductory remarks

In the previous chapters the discussion centered round aspects of clause structure and the morphological elements that appear prefixed to the verb stem in Chichewa. Those elements are more oriented towards aspects of clause structure. It has been argued that they are best analyzed as clitics, since they are syntactic elements that happen to be phonologically bound (cf. Mchombo 2002a). The arguments for analyzing them as clitics will be reviewed below. Clitics are formally and functionally different from the affixes that are suffixed to the verb root. These include affixes that encode passivization, causativization, applicativization, as well as affixes that derive verbs with stative reading and reciprocal verbs. These affixes are traditionally known as extensions. The verbal extensions are functionally different from the clitics in that they affect the number of expressible NPs that the predicate can support. In brief, they are involved in transitivity patterns. They are formally different in that they do not conform to the basic syllable structure of the language. They have a -VC- syllable organization where the language normally requires CV syllable structure. The involvement of verbal extensions in argument structure will be the focus of this chapter.

5.2   The structure of the verb

The verb in Chichewa (and other Bantu languages) is traditionally analyzed as comprising a verb root (VR) to which such verbal extensions as the causative, applicative, reciprocal, passive, etc., are suffixed, and to which prefixes are added. The latter encode information pertaining to agreement with the subject and object(s) of the verb, tense/aspect, negation, modality, etc. Details of the elements that appear prefixed to the VR have been provided above (see chapter 3), together with remarks on their potential to occur with clauses in the subjunctive or non-subjunctive form. Most studies of Bantu languages have focused on verb-stem extensions because of their involvement in argument structure and their potential for reordering, making for interesting questions about the principles underlying verb-stem morphotactics. The fairly rigid order of the prefixal elements has contributed to their marginalization. While work within Bantu scholarship is not likely to see a shift from preoccupation with argument-structure-changing morphology, and recent studies testify to this (cf. Chimbutane 2002; Dlayedwa 2002; Hoffman 1991; Matambirofa 2002; Ngonyani 1996; Simango 1995), some comment on the status of the prefixal elements is in order. We can begin with a restatement of the obvious aspects of the structure of the verb in Bantu. This will be illustrated with data from Chichewa. Consider the following example:

(1)   Mkángo u-da-ómb-án-íts-á   alenje   ndí asodzi.
       3-lion   3SM-pst-hit-recip-caus-fv 2-hunters and 2-fishermen
       'The lion made the hunters and the fishermen hit each other.'

In this, the VR -omb- 'hit' supports the extensions -an- 'reciprocal morpheme' and -its- 'causative,' as well as the prefixes u 'subject marker' and da 'past tense.' Questions pertaining to the status of the morphemes surrounding the VR merit discussion because they are central to the adoption of a specific conception of the morphological structure of the verb in Chichewa (cf. Mchombo 1999a). The structural organization of the verb comprises a subunit – a verb stem, consisting of the VR and the extensions, which constitutes the domain of lexical processes – and the supra-VS material which is oriented towards clause structure and could be analyzed as inflectional morphemes or as clitics. This may also provide an explanation for formal differences between the two.

5.3   Pre-verb-stem morphemes as clitics

We can approach this topic by beginning with issues relating to the distinction between verbal suffixes (extensions) and the verbal prefixes. Although it may amount to prejudicing the issue somewhat, the elements prefixed to the verb stem will be referred to as "clitics." The ensuing account will highlight the substantive issues underlying this terminological preference.

Clitics are generally characterized as independent syntactic constituents which appear phonologically as part of a host word, an attachment characterized by Marantz as "morphological merger," in which "an independent syntactic constituent shows up phonologically as part of a derived word" (Marantz 1988: 253). As independent syntactic constituents, clitic nodes are (base-)generated in structural positions away from the host to which they get attached, but lack "phonological independence." In other words, clitics are syntactic words but not phonologically independent units, perhaps due to failure to satisfy minimality conditions (Jackendoff p.c.). The minimality condition might be the requirement that a phonologically independent word should comprise at least a foot (two syllables). Obvious examples of cliticization are evident in Chichewa, as shown in the data below:

(2) a.   Mbĭdzí   izi   ndi zá   nzĕlu.
          10-zebras 10proxdem be 10SM-assoc 10-intelligence
          'These zebras are intelligent.'

    b.   Mbĭdzí-zi   ndi zá   nzĕlu.
          10-zebras-cltcop be 10SM-assoc 10-intelligence
          'These zebras (the ones already introduced) are intelligent.'

(3)   Mbĭdzí   izo   zí-má-dy-á   maûngu.
          10-zebras 10-distdem 10SM-pstprog-eat-fv 6-pumpkins
          'Those zebras were eating pumpkins.'

(4)   Mkángo u-ma-fúná   ku-séwéla ndí mbĭdzi   koma mbidzí-zo
          3-lion   3SM-pstprog-want inf-play with 10-zebras but 10-zebras-clt
          zi-na-tháwa   chifukwá chá   mântha.
          10SM-pst-escape 7-reason 7SM-assoc 6-fears
          'The lion wanted to play with the zebras but those zebras ran away because of fear.'

(5) a.   Mikángó i-sanu   iyo   i-na-lówá   m'phanga.
          4-lions   4SM-five 4distdem 4SM-pst-enter 16–5-cave
          'Those five lions entered the cave.'

    b.   Mikángó i-sanu-yo   i-na-lówá   m'phanga.
          4-lions   4SM-five-clt 4SM-pst-enter 16–5-cave
          'Those five lions (the ones just referred to) entered the cave.'

(6) a.   Mikángó isanu yóchénjela iyo   i-na-lówá   m'phanga
          4-lions   4-five 4SM-clever 4distdem 4SM-pst-enter 16–5-cave
          'Those five clever lions entered the cave.'

    b.   Mikángó isanu yóchénjéla-yo i-na-lówá   m'phanga.
          4-lions   4-five 4SM-clever-clt 4SM-pst-enter 16-5-cave
          'Those five clever lions (the ones just referred to) entered the cave.'

In these examples, the syntactically independent demonstratives, *izi* 'these,' *izo* 'those,' for class 10 nouns, as well as *iyi* 'these,' and *iyo* 'those' for class 4 nouns, have reduced counterparts, *zi, zo, yi,* and *yo,* with a more anaphoric usage, which do not appear as independent words. Within a noun phrase (NP) configuration the reduced forms appear attached to the immediately preceding full word. These reduced forms, whether attached to NPs or to other syntactic classes, in classical suffixation manner, are called enclitics (cf. Halpern 1998; Poulos 1990). As syntactically independent but phonologically bound elements, "clitics involve a mismatch between the bracketing or structure motivated on semantic and syntactic grounds and the bracketing or structure motivated on phonological grounds" (Marantz 1988). Such mismatches are evident in Chichewa. Consider the data below from textual material:

(7)   Nkhání yá *tsíkúlíyí* idawónjezérá kusafuníká kwá mkúluyu mumtímá mwá
       Sautso koma mnyamatáyó sákadáchítíra mwína.
       'This story of this day increased the undesirability of this guy to Sautso but that
       young man could not do otherwise.'

In this passage, the underlined word *tsíkúliyi* has two clitics, *li* and *yi*, reduced forms of the demonstratives *ili* and *iyi* 'this' for classes 5 and 9 respectively. The NP structure underlying this word is:

[[Nkhání [yá [tsikú ili]]] iyi]
[[9-story [9SM-assoc [5-day 5proxdem]]] 9proxdem]
'This story of this day'

Although the clitic *yi*, by class agreement, is associated with *nkháni* 'story,' it is attached to the full word on its left, which also hosts the other clitic, *li*, which, by agreement too, goes with *tsíku* 'day.'

Below are more instances of cliticization in Chichewa, typical of Bantu languages:

(8)   Mikángó isanu yóchénjélá**yo** inalówá**nsó** mu ndênde ndipó ikusákásáká**bé** afísi
       améné ánábá nyama.
       'Those five clever lions also entered the jail and they are still searching for the
       hyenas which stole the meat.'

The clitic *nso* 'too, also, again, as well,' can be attached to a number of hosts, as exemplified by the following:

(9)   Mkángo ndi nyama yá mthengo komá**nsó** físi nayé**nso** ndi nyama yá
       mthengo**nso**.
       'The lion is a wild animal but also the hyena, it, too, is a wild animal as well.'

(10)   Kalulu wabwela ndí bowa, iwé**nso** wabwelá**nso** ndí zókházókhá**zo**!
       'The hare has brought mushrooms and you too have also come with that same
       stuff!'

The clitic *be* 'still,' while most commonly attached to verbs, can also appear with nominal hosts. Note the following:

(11)   Mtsogoleli akufúfúzá**bé** zá momwé ángáthandizílé asilikáli.
       'The leader is still investigating ways in which s/he can assist the soldiers.'

(12)   Ngakhálé munyinyilĭke, iyé tsópáno ndi mtsogoleli wánú**be**.
       'Although you may grumble, s/he now still remains your leader.'

Bantu languages abound in verbal suffixes, bound morphemes that, in general, are involved in the determination of expressible NP arguments within the sentence. These include the extensions mentioned above. With regard to the variety of extensions in Bantu, various studies provide the relevant samples (Chimbutane 2002; Dembetembe 1987; Dlayedwa 2002; Du Plessis and Visser 1992; Guthrie 1962; Katupha 1991; Matsinhe 1994; Mchombo 1993a, c; Ngunga 2000; Ruge-malira 1993b; Satyo 1985). These, to be reviewed in detail below, include the morphology for encoding the causative, applicative, stative (or neuter), reciprocal, passive, as well as reversive, contactive, and positional (these latter are far less productive now and, in many cases, fused to their host roots). These, together with the verb root, and terminated by the final vowel [a], constitute the verb stem (VS). Constructions involving such extensions are exemplified by the sentences below:

(13)   Mkángo u-na-thyól-á   mpánda.
         3-lion   3SM-pst-break-fv 3-fence
         'The lion broke the fence.'

(14)   Mkángo u-na-thyól-éts-á   mbidzí mpánda.
         3-lion   3SM-pst-break-caus-fv 10-zebras 3-fence
         'The lion made the zebras break the fence.'

(15)   Mkángo u-na-thyól-él-á   mbidzí mpánda.
         3-lion   3SM-pst-break-appl-fv 10-zebras 3-fence
         'The lion broke the fence for the zebras.'

(16)   Mkángo u-na-thyól-éts-él-á   mbidzí mpánda kwá alenje.
         3-lion   3SM-pst-break-caus-appl-fv 10-zebras 3-fence by   2-hunters
         'The lion made the hunters break the fence for the zebras.'

(17)   Mbîdzi   zi-na-thyól-éts-él-édw-á   mpánda kwá alenje
         10-zebras 10SM-pst-break-caus-appl-pass-fv 3-fence by   2-hunters
         (ndí mkángo).
         (by 3-lion)
         'The zebras got the fence broken for (them) by the hunters at the instigation of the lion.'

In these examples, the verb *thyola* 'break' has been extended to form the causative *thyoletsa* 'make break,' the applicative *thyolela* 'break for,' the applicative of a causative *thyoletsela* 'get something broken for someone,' and the passive of the applicativized causative *thyoletseledwa* 'have something broken for one by.' There are morphotactic constraints on the verb stem in Bantu languages (Hyman and Mchombo 1992; Machobane 1993; Ngunga 2000) to be commented upon later. Verbal extensions affect transitivity patterns and are involved in the determination of the argument structure of the predicate (Abasheikh 1978; Alsina 1992, 1993, 1994, 1996a, b; Alsina et al. 1997; Bokamba 1981; Hoffman 1991; Machobane

1989; Mchombo 1997; Ngunga 2000; Satyo 1985; Simango 1995). When the clitics noted above appear together with the verbal extensions, the clitics are attached outside the final vowel. This is demonstrated in (18–22) below:

(18)   Mkángó u-ku-thyól-á-**nsó**   mipando.
         3-lion   3SM-pres-break-fv-too 4-chairs
         'The lion is breaking the chairs too (as well).'

(19)   Mkángó u-ku-thyól-á-**bé**   mipando.
         3-lion   3SM-pres-break-fv-still 4-chairs
         'The lion is still breaking the chairs.'

(20)   Mkángó u-ku-thyól-éts-él-á-**bé**   kalulú mipando kwá físí
         3-lion   3SM-pres-break-caus-appl-fv-still 1a-hare 4-chairs by   1a-hyena
         'The lion is still making the hyena break the chairs for the hare.'

(21)   Mipando i-ku-thyól-édw-á-**nso**.
         4-chairs   4SM-pres-break-pass-fv-too (as well)
         'The chairs are getting broken too (again).'

(22)   Njovu   zi-ku-thyól-éts-él-án-á-**nso**   mipando.
         10-elephants 10SM-pres-break-caus-appl-recip-fv-too 4-chairs
         'The elephants are also getting the chairs broken for each other.'

The relative order of the extensions and the clitics is significant. The extensions appear to be more intimately connected to the host VR, indicated by the fact that the VS is the domain of a number of linguistic processes whose influence does not extend to the suffixed clitics. For instance, there is vowel harmony in Chichewa (Mtenje 1985), in Luganda (Katamba 1984), and many other Bantu languages, but the domain of vowel harmony is, normally, the VS. Further, there are nominalizations that, again, only target the VS (Mchombo 1993b, 1999a). Consider the following:

(23)   kónda   'love'   kóndána 'love each other' chikondano 'mutual love'
         kodza   'urinate'   kodzela 'urinate with'   chikodzelo 'bladder'
         ongola 'straighten' ongolela 'straighten with' chiongolelo 'steering wheel'
         tenga   'take'   tengana 'take each other' mténgáno   'death pact'
         ononga 'damage'   onongéka 'get damaged'   chionongeko 'destruction'
         senda   'skin'   sendédwa 'be skinned'   kasendedwe 'manner of
                                                                     skinning'
         onetsa 'show'   onetsela 'demonstrate'   chionetselo 'exhibition'
         ponda   'step on'   pondela 'step on with'   chipondelo 'soccer cleat
                                                                     (football boot)'

In addition, in Chichewa, verbal reduplication, like vowel harmony, is confined to the VS, excluding the suffixed clitics. This is illustrated below, with the relevant reduplications in boldface:

(24)   Chinkokomo chija **chidakúlílákulilábe**.
        'The rumbling still steadily increased in loudness.'

(25)   Ona zinthu zikunka **zíkuyípíláyipilatu**.
        'Look, things are progressively worsening.'

(26)   Agnes ndí máyí aké ómwe adasángálala ndí mbílíyi pozíndíkila kutí mwína
        kupyólélá mu **zókámbákambazi** zinthu zíkhózá kudzángothélá momwémo
        basi.
        'Agnes and her mother were happy with this rumor recognizing that probably
        through such incessant allegations things might indeed lead to the desired
        conclusion.'

(27)   Masó áwo **ákupónyáponyábe** apa ndí apo m'chipílíngú chá anthu pa dépotípo,
        ine ndidafíká pomwé pánálí atáte.
        'Their eyes still darting back and forth, checking every which way in that crowd
        at the depot, I approached the place where my father was.'

In these examples the enclitics *be* in *chidakúlílákulilábe* and *ákupónyáponyábe*,
tu in *zíkuyípíláyipilatu*, as well as *zi* in *zókámbákambazi*, are excluded from reduplication. The clitics are, thus, treated on a par with the material prefixed to the
VS, but differently from the verbal extensions. The verbal extensions include the
morpheme *-an-* which encodes reciprocity. It, too, participates in reduplication, as
shown below, with the relevant word in boldface:

(28)   Máká ádámúnyánsá adalí máséwélo áke omakóndá **kugwílánágwilana**.
        'What repulsed her particularly was his casual manner of wanting them to
        fondle each other.'

In brief, the VS constitutes the domain of significant linguistic processes that
do not apply to material outside that domain.

5.4   Clitics

The verb stem supports a number of clitics which include the morphology for Tense/Aspect, Subject and Object (agreement) markers, Directional morphemes, Conditional marker, Modal elements, as well as markers for Negation
(NEG), as discussed in the previous chapters. Other languages also have a focus
particle. A rather complex instance of the morphemic organization is exemplified
by the sentence below:

(29)   Sí-ú-kú-ká-ngo-zí-thyóletselá**nso**   mipando.
        neg-3SM-pres-go-just-1OOM-break-caus-appl-too   4-chairs
        'It is not just going to have the chairs broken for them as well (too).'

The prefixed material is exempt from the types of nominalization indicated above, as well as from vowel harmony, reduplication, or involvement with argument-structure changing, etc. In Chichewa the VS has lexical integrity, making it a significant subdomain in the morphological structure of the verb. In previous work the following structural representation of the verb in Chichewa has been proposed:

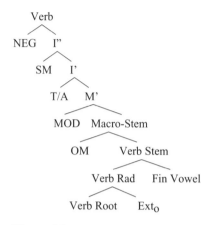

Figure 5.1

In this representation the verb stem is the domain of lexical processes. The supra-verb-stem elements are more oriented to syntactic aspects, somewhat comparable to functional projections within the Principles and Parameters Theory (cf. Chomsky 1991; Pollock 1989). Considerations internal to the functioning of linguistic processes and factors external to, but interacting with or having effects on, the language faculty, seem to support such a structural representation. Let us look at the internal factors.

5.5   On the categorial status of extensions

Verbal extensions in Chichewa can be categorially classified as verbs. The arguments rely, in part, on the analysis of affixes as heads (Marantz 1984; Williams 1981) and, in part, on the endocentricity of the word (Mchombo 1999b). The analysis derives extra credence from diachrony. According to Givón, verbal extensions in Bantu originated as verbs which participated in serial verb constructions, common in the Kwa languages of West Africa, to which the Bantu languages are related. In Bantu these verbs underwent morphologization, reducing them to affixes. Givón points out, further, that some of the verbal prefixes may also have originated as verbs. To account for the constituency of the VS, he advances the hypothesis that their conversion to prefixes or their morphologization occurred at a much later stage. Givón hypothesizes that "[T]here has obviously occurred a considerable time lag between the conversion of the main verbs onto verb suffixes and that of the other main verbs into verb prefixes" (Givón 1971: 157). The diachronic account is intended to explain the involvement of the verbal suffixes in lexical derivation, deriving the VS. The prefixal material, on the other hand, does not participate in lexical derivation. The diachronic account of the differential behavior of verbal suffixes and verbal prefixes is intended to provide a basis for the empirical fact that there is motivation to the verbal organization given above, at least in its identification of the VS as a significant subdomain. The proposal made here is that the prefixal material is not affixal in a sense comparable to that applicable to verbal extensions. Rather, the prefixal elements are clitics, categorially non-verbal, and more involved in the morphosyntactic organization as opposed to the morpholexical aspects characterizing the extensions.

There is more to be said about the status of the pre-VS elements as clitics. Affixes are bound morphemes, constituents of words which occur attached to some host which may itself be free or bound. Haverkort notes that "affixes exhibit a high degree of selection with respect to their stems" (Haverkort 1993: 115). Clitics, on the other hand, while syntactically independent, are phonologically bound, appearing "prosodically bound to an adjacent word" (Halpern 1995: 104). Further, they exhibit a low degree of selection with respect to their hosts.

The property of being bound that characterizes affixes is relevant to the study of pre-verb-stem elements and verbal suffixes (extensions) in Chichewa. The extensions are morphologically bound and, at the level of phonology, they do not satisfy the basic syllable structure or phonotactics of the language. The causative, applicative, passive, stative, and reciprocal extensions in Chichewa are (ignoring variants determined by vowel harmony), respectively, -its-, -il-, -idw-, -ik-, and -an-. Notably, all these have a phonological structure of -VC-, departing from the basic CV syllable structure of the language. In a study of syllable structure of Chichewa, Mtenje argued that "Chichewa syllables are essentially of a CV nature" (Mtenje 1980: 2). In that study Mtenje investigated functional unity or conspiracy of phonological rules in Chichewa which, while independently required, appear to be "primarily motivated by the need to destroy vowel sequences and to reserve the canonical syllable type (CV)" (1980: 18). The verb stem in Chichewa satisfies the syllable structure because of the occurrence of the final vowel, itself analyzed as a separate morpheme. Thus, as noted in chapter 2, the verb stem constitutes a domain with notable non-isomorphism between morphological and phonological structure.

Interestingly, the clitics that appear after the final vowel, attached to the verb stem, invariably have the required phonological structure of CV. Thus, the enclitics *be, tu, zi, nso*, etc. all conform to the syllable structure requirements of the language. In this regard, the elements prefixed to the verb stem, morphemes that have to do with such "functional projections" as NEG, SM, Tense/Aspect, OM, etc. share with the enclitics this conformity to the syllable structure constraints of the language. They all have CV organization. The similarity in phonological structure could, arguably, be accidental and of no material import. Arguments to that effect could be based on the observation that there are morphologically bound prefixes in Chichewa that have the CV syllable structure. For instance, in noun classes both the noun stems and the class prefixes adhere to the CV structure, yet the prefixes are not analyzed as clitics. Further, while clitics are claimed to exhibit a low degree of selection with respect to their hosts, the elements attached to the verb stem seem to exhibit a high degree of selection with respect to their stem, characteristic of affixes, as noted above (Haverkort 1993).

However, the prefixal material and the enclitics do also share the property of appearing outside the VS and, *inter alia*, not getting involved in argument-structure changing, as well as the host of linguistic processes whose domain is the VS. In brief, the similarity may derive from shared fundamental properties. While the prefixal material in the verb structure, treated as functional projections within Principles and Parameters Theory (Chomsky 1991; Chomsky and Lasnik 1993; Laka 1994) lying outside the lexical domain (Pollock 1989), will be designated clitics, oriented more toward syntactic than lexical organization, the issue of whether they are simply prefixes is one that is noted and may need to be addressed further. In brief, the VS in Chichewa comprises a structural domain separating morpholexical from morphosyntactic operations. For further comment on the distinction between morpholexical and morphosyntactic operations, see Sadler and Spencer (1998). This structural analysis of Chichewa has been vehemently argued for within an autosegmental and Lexical Phonology-theoretic framework (Mtenje 1985).

5.6   Clitics and inflectional morphology

The position adopted here is reminiscent of the traditional distinction between inflectional and derivational morphology (cf. Anderson 1988), apparently supporting the split morphology hypothesis (Perlmutter 1988). The specialization of the VS to lexical processes while the morphology outside that domain is oriented toward the non-lexical aspects of linguistic structure is underscored by the tendency within various theoretical frameworks to, at the minimum, acknowledge the special status of the VS. For instance, Givón, couching his analysis within the framework of the "standard theory" version of transformational grammar (Chomsky 1965), derived the VS through applications of the transformational rule of predicate raising. This is a rule that affected the verb of an embedded sentence and "raised and adjoined to the one from the higher sentence – which then becomes, in Bantu, a suffix. This format is at present controversial, but regardless of one's position with regard to it, I would like to claim that the semantic facts seem to suggest a verbal origin of the Bantu suffixes" (1971: 152). The rule of predicate raising was eventually analyzed as precyclic, and precyclic transformations were claimed to be presyntactic (Newmeyer 1974, 1975). The VS was, thus, not syntactically derived. Of course Givón also attributed the integrity of the VS to aspects of diachrony, as noted above.

The analysis offered by Givón has echoes in work within Principles and Parameters Theory. Baker proposes to account for the creation of the VS through the process of incorporation, an aspect of head movement, constrained by the Head Movement Constraint (Baker 1988a; Marantz 1988; Sproat 1988; Travis 1984). In the incorporation analysis there is (head) movement of the affixal heads of Causative, Applicative, etc., to the predicate of the higher or matrix clause. This is the case with the applicative. With regard to the causative, the causative affix may itself be taken to be the higher (affixal) predicate CAUSE (*-its-* in Chichewa) to which the predicate of the embedded proposition is moved (cf. Abasheikh 1978). Either way the derivation involves predicate raising. The incorporation analysis of the formation of VS, very much like the predicate raising approach of Givón, of which it is a variant in relevant respects, reduces to the recognition of the VS as a domain of lexical processes. Note that the rule of predicate raising is not implicated in the morphologization of the material outside the VS.

In the Lexical Syntax approach of Hale and Keyser (cf. Hale and Keyser 1992), extended to Chichewa (and Bantu) by Hoffman, the VS is the domain of l-syntax processes. In Lexical Phonology and Morphology-theoretic approaches or level-ordered morphology (Kiparsky 1982a, b; Mohanan 1986; Mtenje 1986b) the VS constitutes the domain of level 1 rules, with the clitics coming in at level 2 (or later) processes. These approaches subsume, or extend to, the analysis adopted by Klavans (1983), whose distinction between lexical clitics and postlexical clitics, interacting in a manner consistent with the stipulations and organization of level-ordered morphology, reduces to no more than terminological innovation or preference. In brief, within every framework, various processes converge on a unit comparable to the VS in Chichewa, giving it a distinctive character that argues for its uniqueness or lexical integrity. The inescapable conclusion is that the prefixal material is more involved in the morphosyntactic organization of the expression. In fact, Baker remarks, with regard to Mohawk, that "pronominal morphology is clearly a subtype of inflectional morphology, whereas noun incorporation is more similar to derivational morphology" (Baker 1990: 27). Could clitics in Chichewa be reduced to inflectional morphemes?

The identification of clitics with inflectional morphemes is a vexed question, resolved within specific theories of inflectional morphology. It is also determined by the views maintained about the nature of clitics in linguistic theory. Everett (1989) makes the claim that all clitics and inflectional affixes are syntactically the same type of element, differing only in their requirements for morphological or phonological support. In Chichewa the question of whether elements prefixed to the verb stem are best analyzed as clitics or as inflectional morphemes could reduce to terminological preference (Roberge 1990). As noted in the preceding section, the prefix/clitic analysis could go either way. The real issue is that the morphological structure of the verb in Chichewa makes for a principled distinction between the domain characterized by the VS and the larger structure in which the VS is embedded. In this work the elements prosodically associated with, but not contained within, the VS, will be called clitics. They could equally be designated inflectional morphemes without affecting the analysis in any way. This is the terminology adopted by Kula (2002). She notes that "[S]uffixation in Bantu generally involves derivational affixes although some inflectional suffixes, such as the perfect do occur" (Kula 2002: 107). Focusing on phonological domains she claims that "[T]he distinction between inflectional versus derivational suffixes is irrelevant for determining phonological domains" (ibid).

In other domains the distinction may be relevant. Continuing with the designation of clitics for the morphemes attached to the verb stem, those that attach to, or form a prosodic unit with, a host on their right, are proclitics. These include the SM and OM, elements analyzed as incorporated pronominal arguments in Bantu (Bentley 1994; Bresnan and Mchombo 1986, 1987; Demuth and Johnson 1989; Keach 1995). This appears to assimilate these languages to the pronominal argument hypothesis, accounting for aspects of word order (Jelinek 1984; Neale 1996), among other things. The consequences of that have been discussed in the previous chapter. There, it was noted that the SM and OM satisfy the requirements of argument structure of the VS and have implications for discontinuity of the constituents of the nominal adjuncts in agreement with them.

Assuming the correctness of this analysis, grammatical theory should provide the architecture for capturing the formal and functional differences associated with the morphology of the verb in Bantu, as well as facilitating explanation of the structural organization of the verb. Grammatical theory should, therefore, provide for capturing aspects of argument structure which, in Chichewa, seem to be localized within the VS; aspects of functional structure, to which such elements as NEG, Tense/Aspect, SM, OM, etc. make some contribution; and the overt realization of these components in the verbal morphology. Again, without going into the technical details of the theory, the architecture and technical apparatus, the theory of LFG is germane to meeting the stated requirements.

5.7   Argument structure and the verb stem

The most engaging aspect of Bantu verbal morphology lies in the verbal suffixes that also affect the number of NPs that the verb can "support" in the syntactic configuration. The suffixes can be conveniently subdivided into three groups:

(i)   those that increase by one the number of NPs that can appear in the sentence

(ii)   those that reduce by a corresponding amount the number of NPs the suffixed or extended verb can support

(iii)   those that do not alter the array of NPs.

In correlation with these properties Guthrie (1962) classifies the extensions as O+, O–, and neutral (where O is really for "object"). Typical examples of the O+ extensions are the causative and applicative morphemes; O– extensions are exemplified by the stative, passive, and reciprocal morphemes. The "neutral" is shown by the reversive. The suffixes constitute argument-structure-changing morphology. In this chapter we will discuss those morpholexical processes that affect the argument structure by increasing by one the number of expressible NPs. These are the causative and the applicative extensions. The extensions that reduce by one the number of NPs that can be associated with primary grammatical functions, as well as those that are neutral, will be discussed in the next chapter.

5.8   The causative

It is practically impossible to do justice to the topic of causatives in view of the degree of scholarly attention that causativization has received. The sustained attention derives from the range of problems associated with the description and analysis of the facts about causative constructions. The causative in Chichewa is realized by the morphs -its- and -ets-, the choice of the morph being determined by vowel harmony (cf. Mtenje 1985, 1986b). The causative morpheme is suffixed to the verb with the result that there is a new NP introduced into the structure. Consider the following examples illustrating causativization of an intransitive verb:

(30) a.   Chigawênga   chi-ku-sêk-a.
            7-terrorist   7SM-pres-laugh-fv
            'The terrorist is laughing.'

    b.   Kalulú   a-ku-sék-éts-á   chigawênga.
            1a-hare   1SM-pres-laugh-caus-fv   7-terrorist
            'The hare is making the terrorist laugh.'

The presence of the causative suffix *-ets-* is accompanied by the introduction of a new NP *kalŭlu* 'hare,' into the structure. This new NP assumes the function of grammatical subject. The causativization of a transitive verb is shown in (31) below:

(31) a. Mkángó u-ku-phwány-íts-á   chigawéngá maûngu.
         3-lion 3SM-pres-smash-caus-fv 7-terrorist 6-pumpkins
         'The lion is making the terrorist smash pumpkins.'

In this sentence the presence of the suffix *-its-* is accompanied by the introduction of the NP *mkángó*. This NP would not otherwise have appeared in the construction, as shown below:

   b. *Mkángó u-ku-phwány-á   chigawéngá maûngu.
       *3-lion 3SM-pres-smash-fv 7-terrorist 6-pumpkins

The subject NP of the non-causative construction no longer appears as subject in the causative construction. Chichewa provides two strategies for the realization of the subject of the non-causative sentence when the input structure is transitive. It can appear either as the object NP, as in (31) above, or as an oblique, marked by *kwá* as shown in (32) below:

(32) Mkángó u-ku-phwány-íts-á   maúngú   kwá chigawônga.
      3-lion 3SM-pres-smash-caus-fv 6-pumpkins by 7-terrorist
      'The lion is getting pumpkins smashed at the hands of (by) the terrorist.'

These two versions of the causative have semantic differences. First, when the causee surfaces as the object, the causative is "direct." In sentence (31) the lion must be making the terrorist smash the pumpkins. In sentence (32), on the other hand, the lion is merely having pumpkins smashed at the hands of the terrorist. The idea of direct force is not a necessary part of its interpretation. The causative is one of the extensions that increase the number of allowable overt arguments by one. The other extension that has received widespread attention is the applicative. These two extensions have traditionally been central to studies of double-object constructions (cf. Abasheikh 1978; Alsina 1992; Alsina and Joshi 1991; Hoffman 1991; Matambirofa 2002; Ngonyani 1996; Rugemalira 1993b, to name only a few).

The causative is also manifested in other ways besides the affixation of *-its-*. As noted by Simango (1999), the affix *-ts* is attached to verbs with a stem-final /k/, whereas the affix *-z* is attached to verbs with a stem-final liquid. These are shown in the data below:

(33)   Base form   Causativized form
        tuluk-a 'come out'   tuluts-a 'bring out'
        ulúk-a   'fly'   uluts-a   'fly (transitive)'
        olok-a   'cross (river)'   olots-a   'make cross'
        chok-a   'leave, depart'   chots-a   'remove'
        lék-a   'stop, quit'   lets-a   'stop, forbid'
        kwel-a   'climb'   kwez-a   'hoist'
        míl-a   'drown, sink'   miz-a   'drown (transitive)'
        lil-a   'cry'   liz-a   'ring, make cry'
        kul-a   'grow big'   kuz-a   'enlarge'
        vulál-a 'be injured'   vulaz-a   'injure'
        pol-a   'cool off'   poz-a   'cool something'

In these cases the base verbs describe autonomous events while the causative forms involve the intervention of an agent, describing externally caused eventualities. Simango maintains that such causatives "describe situations in which an animate being performs an action that leads to the main event" (Simango 1999: 72). Simango labels these causatives as Type I, contrasting them with the productively derived causative verbs formed through the affixation of -its-. These latter he classifies as Type II. The major difference between the two types is that Type I causatives only have the direct causation reading whereas Type II causatives allow for indirect causation reading too. Such patterns are attested in other languages and Simango draws from data in Chinsenga, another Bantu language, closely related to, and most likely a dialect variation of, Chichewa.

The major thrust of Simango's typology of the causatives is the desire to motivate a lexical as well as syntactic analysis of causatives. The causatives involving the affix -its- are, for him, syntactically derived. On the other hand, Type I causatives are lexically derived. They even manifest the non-productivity characteristic of lexical derivation. Thus, there are verbs with /k/ stem endings or stems ending with liquids that fail to be causativized with the -ts or -z forms, deleting or replacing the /k/ or the liquid. This is illustrated by the following:

(34)   kok-a   'pull'   *kots-a
        sok-a   'sew'   *sots-a
        luk-a   'weave'   *luts-a
        pal-a   'scrape'   *paz-a
        kal-a   'scratch'   *kaz-a
        kolol-a 'harvest'   *koloz-a
        bal-a   'give birth'   *baz-a
        kol-a   'trip'   *koz-a

Type I causative affixes seem to attach to verbs in an idiosyncratic and unpredictable manner and, in some languages, they can also alter the shape of the stem to which they attach through phonological modification. For instance, op-a 'be afraid' has the causatives -opsa or ofya 'frighten.' It should be noted that Chichewa has the verbs -*paza* 'pass, go via' and *koz-a* 'fix, repair, prepare' but these have nothing to do with the causatives of *pal-a* 'scrape,' or *kol-a* 'trip, catch in a trap.' Type II causatives, on the other hand, are more regular, productive, and their behavior is characteristic of syntactic processes.

Countering this argument in detail is not easy at this juncture. While Simango's proposal is attractive, it still fails to undermine the lexical analysis of causatives. Among the arguments against a syntactic analysis of Type II causatives is their ability to feed the applicative and the reciprocal, both demonstrably lexical processes (cf. Mchombo 1978, 1980; Mchombo and Ngalande 1980), as well as their participation in such lexical processes as reduplication and nominalization (cf. Mchombo 1993b). While noting that the issue of the syntactic analysis of causatives is likely to remain alive, the view will still be maintained here that causatives are part of lexical derivation.

5.9   The applicative

The applicative construction in Chichewa is typified by the suffixation of -*il*- or -*el*- to the verb, with the consequence that a new NP is introduced into the construction. Consider the following:

(35) a.   Kalulú   a-ku-phík-á   maûngu.
          1a-hare 13M-pres-cook-fv   6-pumpkins
          'The hare is cooking pumpkins.'

     b.   Kalulú   a-ku-phík-íl-á   mkángó maûngu.
          1a-hare 1SM-pres-cook-appl-fv 3-lion   6-pumpkins
          'The hare is cooking (for) the lion some pumpkins.'

The most obvious difference between the causative and the applicative has to do with the semantic roles and the grammatical functions associated with the new NP. In causative constructions the new NP is agentive and is normally realized as the grammatical subject of the sentence. The applicative, on the other hand, introduces non-agentive NPs. These are not directly associated with the subject function. In (35b) above, the applied argument (NP) *mkángó*, is introduced as the direct object and it is associated with the semantic role of beneficiary. The applicative construction is complex in that the NP associated with the presence of the applied suffix can be associated with a number of semantic roles. We can proceed to examine the issue.

Along with the causative, the applicative is involved in the creation of double-object constructions. In recent studies of double-object constructions in Bantu, attention has focused on questions relating to (a) the nature of postverbal noun phrases that appear to act as objects in applicative or causative sentences; (b) the status of the applicative and causative verbal suffixes, either as head predicators or as argument-structure-changing suffixes operating in the lexical component of the theory of grammar (cf. Alsina 1993; Baker 1988b; Hoffman 1991).

Double-object constructions in Bantu can be illustrated by sentences like the following from Swahili:

(36) a. Mwalimu a-li-pik-a   ndizi.
          1-teacher 1SM-pst cook-fv 10-bananas
          'The teacher cooked bananas.'

     b. Mwalimu a-li-pik-i-a   watoto   ndizi.
          1-teacher 1SM-pst-cook-appl-fv 2-children 10-bananas
          'The teacher cooked the children some bananas.'

Sentence (36b) differs from (36a) in at least two ways. First, the verb *pik-a* 'cook' has been modified by suffixation to become *pik-i-a* 'cook for.' This verbal suffixation has traditionally been called the applicative. In Swahili, the applicative is marked by the verbal suffix *-i-* or *-e-* while in other Bantu languages it is marked by forms such as *-il-*, *-el-* (e.g. Chichewa), *-el-* (e.g. Gitonga, classified by Guthrie as S62, or Changana, classified as S53), or cognates of those. Secondly, sentence (36b) has two noun phrases following the verb. The presence of one of the noun phrases is clearly licensed by the applied suffix, as evidenced by the ungrammaticality of sentence (36c) below, in which the verb is followed by the two noun phrases but it has not been modified through the addition of the applicative suffix:

     c. *Mwalimu a-li-pik-a   watoto   ndizi
          1-teacher 1SM-pst-cook-fv 2-children 10-bananas

The attention accorded to the postverbal noun phrases in such constructions has revolved around their status with respect to objecthood. To put it simply, do these postverbal NPs bear the same grammatical relations to the verb or are they different? Different Bantu languages seem to offer different answers to this question. For instance, de Guzman (1987) points out that in Siswati, the NPs found in such ditransitive constructions must be distinguished because they have variable behavior. De Guzman argues against the "two object analysis" proposed by Gary and Keenan (1977) for Kinyarwanda. In the "two object analysis," the claim is that the postverbal NPs behave alike in all relevant aspects. Bresnan and Moshi (1990) deal with languages which provide evidence for these conflicting views and propose to derive the differences from a single parameter which they designate the "Asymmetrical Object Parameter (AOP)." Languages such as Kinyarwanda and Kichaga, for which the "two object analysis" appears to hold, have been called "symmetric languages," whereas languages such as Chichewa and Siswati in which the NPs behave differently are referred to as "asymmetric languages." Some languages (e.g. Sesotho) seem to be of mixed types in that they have both asymmetric and symmetric object marking, depending on semantic roles (see Alsina 1993, for relevant discussion).

The applicative construction in Chichewa is used to introduce into the argument structure of the verb nominal expressions that have the semantic role of beneficiary, as well as instruments, locative, and circumstantial (cf. Hyman and Mchombo 1992) or malefactive (cf. Mchombo 1993c). The beneficiary applicative appears to be both historically and cross-linguistically the primary function of the applicative morpheme in Bantu languages (cf. Trithart 1983) in that, for every language that has the applicative, it is likely to encode a beneficiary or benefactive argument. Other languages extend the use of the applicative to encode instrumentals or locatives.

The characterization of a language as symmetric or asymmetric in Bantu derives from the behavior of the postverbal NPs in double-object constructions with respect to, *inter alia*, the following tests:

a.   word order
b.   passivizability
c.   cliticization
d.   reciprocalization
e.   wh-extraction.

Comments on the utility of these tests follow. The test of word order reduces to the question of whether the postverbal NPs have comparable potential for string adjacency with the verb. In other words, could the two NPs that follow the verb be freely ordered such that any one of them appears immediately after the verb without altering either the grammaticality or the meaning of the sentence? In asymmetric languages, the two NPs do not have comparable access to the immediate postverbal position. This is shown by the following sentences from Chichewa:

(37) a.   Alenje   a-ku-phík-á   zítúmbûwa.
          2-hunters 2SM-pres-cook-fv 8-pancakes
          'The hunters are cooking pancakes.'

     b.   Alenje   a-ku-phík-íl-á   anyaní   zítúmbûwa.
          2-hunters 2SM-pres-cook-appl-fv 2-baboons 8-pancakes
          'The hunters are cooking (for) the baboons some pancakes.'

     c.   *Alenje   a-ku-phík-íl-á   zitumbúwá anyani.
          2-hunters 2SM-pres-cook-appl-fv 8-pancakes 2-baboons

A reversal of the ordering of the postverbal NPs given in (37b) renders the output ungrammatical, as sentence (37c) illustrates. In this example, the applicative is associated with the introduction of an NP that has the semantic role of beneficiary. The NP that bears the beneficiary role must occur immediately after the verb, preceding the NP that bears the patient or theme role. This ordering is only reversed when the object marker (OM) which agrees with the beneficiary NP is included within the verbal morphology, as shown in (37d) below:

> d. Alenje   a-ku-wá-phík-íl-á   zítúmbûwa anyâni.
>   2-hunters 2SM-pres-2OM-cook-appl-fv 8-pancakes 2-baboons
>   'The hunters are cooking for them (the baboons) some pancakes.'

In this example, the OM *wá* replaces or, rather, agrees with the beneficiary NP *anyâni* 'baboons.' The OM, an incorporated pronominal argument, satisfies the argument-structure requirements of the predicate, making the NP it is in agreement with a discourse-licensed extra-sentential NP. This status of the NP is overtly signaled in part by the word-order reflexes in that the NP is ordered outside the verb phrase (VP) and, indeed, outside the sentence (for relevant observations, cf. de Guzman 1987). This is also the case with the ordering of the object NPs in benefactive-applicative constructions in Changana, when the incorporated pronominal object marked is included in the verbal morphology (cf. Chimbutane 2002).

In a typical symmetrical language, the verb with an applicative suffix can have either one of the postverbal NPs adjacent to it without inducing changes to either grammaticality or meaning (cf. Bresnan and Moshi 1990).

5.10   Passivizability

Passivization in Bantu languages is comparable to English or other languages in that the subject NP of the sentence in the active voice is either eliminated or expressed by an oblique function and the object NP assumes the functional role of subject, with attendant morphological modification of the verb. For instance, the passive of sentence (37a) above is given in (38) below, where the passive morphology in Chichewa is marked by the verbal suffix *-idw-*:

(38)   Maúngu   a-ku-phík-ídw-a   (ndí álenje).
        6-pumpkins 6SM-pres-cook-pass-fv (by 2-hunters)
        'The pumpkins are being cooked (by the hunters).'

In double-object constructions in Bantu languages the question is whether the postverbal NPs can both be targets for assignment of the subject function under passivization. Again, in an asymmetric language such as Chichewa, the response is in the negative. Only the beneficiary can be assigned the subject function under passivization. Consider the following, which are different passivizations of sentence (37b) above:

(39) a. Anyaní   a-ku-phík-íl-idw-á   maúngu   (ndí álenje).
          2-baboons 2SM-pres-cook-appl-pass-fv 6-pumpkins (by hunters)
          'The baboons are being cooked pumpkins (by the hunters).'
     b. *Maúngu   a-ku-phík-íl-idw-á   anyâni   (ndí álenje).
          6-pumpkins 2SM-pres-cook-appl-pass-fv 2-baboons (by 2-hunters)

5.11   Cliticization

It has been noted that included in the verbal morphology in Bantu languages are clitics that are prefixed to the verb stem. In Chichewa, the OM clitic has been analyzed as an incorporated pronominal which is anaphorically linked to a discourse-licensed extra-sentential NP. Chichewa only permits one OM in the verbal morphology. Chichewa also permits the doubling of the OM with the NP with which it is in agreement, characteristic of clitic-doubling as noted in Romance languages (cf. Jaeggli 1982; Roberge 1990). There are other languages in which such doubling is not permitted, so that the OM is in complementary distribution with the object NP. This has been noted in Kikuyu (cf. Bergvall 1985; Mugane 1997).

Other languages, for instance, Kichaga, Kinyarwanda, and Runyambo, allow more than one OM and, as a consequence, these languages have sometimes been referred to as double- or multiple-object-marking languages (cf. Bresnan and Moshi 1990; Kimenyi 1980; Rugemalira 1991, 1993a). This means that in such languages sentences comparable to (40) below, in which the two postverbal NPs have their respective OMs included in the verbal morphology, are grammatical, something that is not possible in Chichewa.

(40) a. *Alenje   a-ku-zí-wá-phík-il-a   (zítúmbûwa anyâni).
          2-hunters 2SM-pres-8OM-2OM-cook-appl-fv 8-pancakes 2-baboons
          'The hunters are cooking them (the pancakes) for them (the baboons).'
     b. *Alenje   a-ku-wá-zí-phík-il-a   (zítúmbûwa anyâni).
          2-hunters 2SM-pres-2OM-8OM-cook-appl-fv 8-pancakes 2-baboons
          'The hunters are cooking them (the baboons) for them (the pancakes).'

The relevance of object marking, which we have termed cliticization here, to the status of the postverbal NPs in double-object constructions reduces to whether either one of the NPs can be anaphorically linked to the OM. In Chichewa, the response is, once again, in the negative. In a beneficiary applicative, only the beneficiary NP can have its features expressed by an OM (cf. sentence (37b) above). Note the following:

(41) a. Alenje   a-ku-wá-phík-il-á   zítúmbûwa (anyáni).
          2-hunters 2SM-pres-2OM-cook-appl-fv 8-pancakes (2-baboons)
          'The hunters are cooking (for) them (the baboons) some pancakes.'
     b. *Alenje   a-ku-zí-phík-il-á   anyáni   (zítúmbûwa).
          2-hunters 2SM-pres-8OM-cook-appl-fv 2-baboons (8-pancakes)

Sentence (41b) is grammatical with the reading that the hunters are cooking the baboons for the pancakes. Again these sentences show the variable behavior of the postverbal NPs with respect to cliticization or object marking in Chichewa. This is again typical of the situation in asymmetric languages.

5.12   Reciprocalization

In Bantu languages the formation of verbs with reciprocal reading or conveying the idea of reciprocity is effected through the suffixation of the form -an- to the verb root or verb stem. Such verbs do not take direct objects, as can be shown by their failure to co-occur with an OM in monotransitive constructions in those languages that do not allow double-object marking. This can be shown by the following Chichewa examples:

(42) a. Alenje   a-ku-tém-an-a.
          2-hunters 2SM-pres-cut-recip-fv
          'The hunters are cutting each other.'
     b. *Alenje   a-ku-wá-tém-an-a.
          2-hunters 2SM-pres-2OM-cut-recip-fv

Furthermore, the reciprocal cannot co-occur with the passive in a basic underived or unextended verb. Consider

     c. *Alenje   a-ku-tém-án-idw-a.
          2-hunters 2SM-pres-cut-recip-pass-fv

The facts about the reciprocals seem to be consistent with the analysis of the reciprocal as an argument-structure-changing operation that has a detransitivizing effect. The noted incompatibility between reciprocal verbs and OMs or passive morphology derives from the intransitive nature of the verb (cf. Mchombo 1992; Mchombo and Ngunga 1994). If, on the other hand, the verb root is extended with the reciprocal and the causative morphemes, in either order, then the passive can co-occur with the reciprocal. This is illustrated by the following:

(43) a.   Alenje   a-ku-tém-án-íts-ídw-á   (ndí mikángo).
        2-hunters 2SM-pres-cut-recip-caus-pass-fv (by 4-lions).
        'The hunters are being made to cut each other (by the lions).'

    b.   Alenje   a-ku-tém-éts-án-ídw-á   (ndí mikángo).
        2-hunters 2SM-pres-cut-caus-recip-pass-fv (by 4-lions)
        'The hunters are being forced to make each other cut (by the lions).'

It could be argued that instead of treating -an- as a detransitivizing suffix, it should itself be viewed as an argument that is incorporated into the verb. Taken as such, -an- would be comparable to its English equivalent 'each other' which does have the distribution of an argument and could thus be analyzed as an incorporated pronominal along the lines suggested for the analysis of the OM (Bresnan and Mchombo 1986, 1987). In fact, such a treatment of the reciprocal morpheme in Bantu languages is implicit in the following remark by Guthrie:

> although the element -an- is in every respect an extension, it can be regarded as replacing the direct object of the simplex radical. The main feature that distinguishes verbals containing this extension is the limitation of the subject to nominals in classes expressing a plural meaning.   (Guthrie 1962: 96)

This particular remark does not in and of itself argue for the treatment of the suffix -an- as the object argument. However, Guthrie appears to openly espouse this view, as evidenced by the closing remarks of the work quoted above. Commenting on co-occurrence possibilities among the extensions he makes the claim that

> [O]ccasionally two extensions can occur together in either order but with a different meaning in each case, as in Kongo -fing-/ -fingisan-/ -finganis- 'curse'/ 'cause one another to curse'/ 'cause to curse one another.' In this case the second radical can support an object which refers to the simplex, while the extension -an- serves as the direct object of the extension -is- causative, the third radical, however, can support an object referring to -is- causative, since the extension -an- serves as the direct object of the simplex.   (Guthrie 1962: 110).

A similar analysis is advanced by Abasheikh (1978).

Kinyalolo (1991), on the other hand, makes the claim that the reciprocal is an r-expression, i.e. a referring expression in the sense of the binding theory module of the theory of Government and Binding (GB) (Chomsky 1981). Kinyalolo does not provide any arguments for this analysis that are based on distributional criteria. Despite Guthrie's remarks, as well as those of the others cited, the available evidence points in the direction of either the derivational nature of the reciprocal morpheme (Mchombo and Ngunga 1994) or a radically different analysis. While more evidence about the non-argument status of the reciprocal morpheme in Bantu has been documented in studies of binding in Bantu languages (Alsina

1993; Mchombo and Ngalande 1980), there is one argument that can be exploited here to lend further support to this analysis. This has to do with the co-occurrence of the OM with the reciprocal verb.

In such languages as Emakhuwa and Swahili (cf. Katupha 1991; Omar 1990), the OM has increasingly come to be reanalyzed as a regular grammatical agreement marker when the object is animate, in that its occurrence tends to be obligatory. In these languages the occurrence of the OM merely signals grammatical agreement with the object argument. Some factors seem to be consistent with such an analysis, for instance, the fact that the presence of the OM does not induce dislocation of the object NP. If the reciprocal suffix is analyzed as an incorporated argument then it would be predicted that its co-occurrence with the OM should not yield ungrammatical results in those languages – yet it does. Consider the following sentence from Swahili:

(44)   *Simba   wa-li-wa-pig-an-a.
        10-lions 2SM-pst-2OM-hit-recip-fv

The sentence is ungrammatical because of the presence of the OM *wa*. This is readily explained if it is realized that the form *pigana* 'hit each other' is intransitive, hence it cannot support an agreement marker for a non-existent and impermissible object argument. Such an analysis of the reciprocal as a detransitivizing morpheme is consistent with the distributional properties of this suffix. Note that in Bantu, argument-structure-changing processes are ordinarily morphologically encoded by verbal suffixes. An analysis of the reciprocal as an incorporated argument would fail to provide an explanation for its form as a suffix and its interaction with the suffixes that are morphological exponents of argument-structure-changing operations. We will maintain that the reciprocal is a detransitivizing morpheme and that it eliminates the object noun phrase or, at the minimum, that it is not a syntactic argument (for illuminating discussion and a proposal that may suggest otherwise, cf. Seidl and Dimitriadis 2003). The issue will be taken up further in the next chapter.

The issue now is that of determining which of the NPs in a double-object construction counts as the object under reciprocalization. Again, in Chichewa only the beneficiary NP can be eliminated. For example:

(45)   Anyaní   a-na-gúl-íl-an-a   uchéma.
        2-baboons 2SM-pst-buy-appl-recip-fv 14-palm wine
        'The baboons bought one another some palm wine.'

The second NP *uchéma* 'palm wine' is completely inaccessible as a target for reciprocalization. Chichewa, once again, turns out to be asymmetric.

5.13   Extraction

The formation of cleft constructions in Chichewa has been discussed in chapter 4. It was noted that it parallels that of English in that the topicalized NP is fronted and either there is a gap in the pre-movement site or there is an OM functioning as a resumptive pronoun. Consider the following:

(46) a.   Anyaní   a-na-b-á   maûngu.
            2-baboons 2SM-pst-steal-fv 6-pumpkins
            'The baboons stole some pumpkins.'

     b.   Awa   ndi maúngú   améné   anyaní   á-ná-b-a.
            6-these be 6-pumpkins 6SM-rel 2-baboons 2SM-pst-steal-fv
            'These are the pumpkins that the baboons stole.'

In double-object constructions in Chichewa the postverbal NPs are differently affected by such wh-extraction. It turns out that the extraction of the beneficiary NP is disallowed, while the fronting of the patient NP yields grammatical results, thus manifesting variable treatment of the object NPs by the extraction process. For instance,

(47) a.   Anyani   a-na-phík-íl-á   mbúzí   chítúmbûwa.
            2-baboons 2SM-pst-cook-appl-fv 10-goats 7-pancake
            'The baboons cooked (for) the goats a pancake.'

     b.   Ichi   ndi chitumbúwá chi-méné anyaní   á-ná-phík-íl-a   mbûzi.
            7-this be 7-pancake   7SM-rel 2-baboons 2SM-pst-cook-appl-fv 10-goats
            'This is the pancake that the baboons cooked for the goats.'

     c.   *Izi   ndi mbúzí   zi-méné anyaní   á-ná-phík-íl-a
            10-these be 10-goats 10SM-rel 2-baboons 2SM-pst-cook-appl-fv
            chítúmbûwa.
            7-pancake
            'These are the goats that the baboons cooked the pancake for.'

This last sentence becomes grammatical if the OM agreeing with *mbûzi* 'goats' is included in the verbal morphology. Thus, the sentence below is grammatical:

     d.   Izi   ndi mbúzí   zi-méné anyaní   á-ná-zí-phík-íl-a
            10-these be 10-goats 10SM-rel 2-baboons 2SM-pst-10OM-cook-appl-fv
            chítúmbûwa.
            7-pancake
            'These are the goats that the baboons cooked the pancake for.'

Or consider the following:

     e.   Kalulú   a-na-lémb-él-á   chitsílu kálata.
            1a-hare 1SM-pst-write-appl-fv 7-fool   9-letter
            'The hare wrote the fool a letter = the hare wrote a letter to/for the fool.'

f. *Ichi ndi chitsílu chi-méné   kalulú a-na-lémb-él-á   kálata.
    7-this be   7-fool   7SM-relpro 1a-hare 1SM-pst-write-appl-fv 9-letter

g. Ichi   ndi chitsílu chi-méné   kalulú a-na-**chí**-lémb-él-á   kálata.
    7-this be   7-fool   7SM-relpro 1a-hare 1SM-pst-**7OM**-write-appl-fv 9-letter
    'This is the fool that the hare wrote a letter to/for.'

The inclusion of the OM that agrees with the applied object, with the OM functioning as a resumptive pronoun, improves the grammaticality of the sentence, as shown in (47g).

The facts presented show that the postverbal NPs in double-object constructions in Chichewa behave differently with respect to various grammatical tests. Chichewa thus emerges as a very clear case of an asymmetric language. The asymmetric object parameter embodies very specific proposals about the factors underlying the argument asymmetries in languages such as Chichewa and the apparent lack of asymmetries in languages such as Kichaga.

5.14   Instrumental and locative applicatives

The applicative is also used to introduce instrumental as well as locatives into the range of arguments that the predicate can support. Note the following:

Instrumental applicative

(48) a. Kalúlú a-ku-phík-á   maúngú   ndí mkóndo.
         1a-hare 1SM-pres-cook-fv 6-pumpkins with 3-spear
         'The hare is cooking pumpkins with (using) a spear.'

     b. Kalúlú a-ku-phík-íl-á   mkóndo maûngu.
         1a-hare 1SM-pres-cook-appl-fv 3-spear 6-pumpkins
         'The hare is cooking pumpkins with a spear.'

In this the instrumental argument *mkóndo* 'spear' behaves like the object of the applied verb *phik-il-a*.

Locative applicative

(49) a. Kalulú a-ku-phík-á   maûngu   pa   chulu.
         1a-hare 1SM-pres-cook-fv 6-pumpkins 16-on 7-anthill
         'The hare is cooking some pumpkins on the anthill.'

     b. Kalulú a-ku-phík-íl-a   pa   chulu maûngu.
         1a-hare 1SM-pres-cook-appl-fv 16-on 7-anthill 6-pumpkins
         'The hare is cooking on the anthill the pumpkins.'

In these examples the resultant sentences show some of the hallmarks of double-object constructions (but see Alsina and Mchombo 1990, 1991, for important observations).

Circumstantial applicative

The applicative is further utilized to introduce a reason or purpose NP, which has also been referred to as the circumstantial (cf. Hyman and Mchombo 1992). This is shown in the following sentence:

(50) a.   Kalulú a-ku-phík-íl-a   njala   maûngu.
          1a-hare 1SM-pres-cook-appl-fv 9-hunger 6-pumpkins
          'The hare is cooking the pumpkins because of hunger.'

This sentence says that the hare is cooking the pumpkins because of hunger. There are constraints on word order in this case. The reordering of *maûngu* before *njala* yields ungrammatical results. Besides, the applied argument *njala* lacks the characteristics of a true object, according to the diagnostics given above. It cannot control the OM, neither can it be the subject under passivization.

In this the circumstantial NP differs from the theme NP which can control object marking. Consider the following:

b.   Ndí-ma-dy-él-á   njala   maûngu.
     1st sing-hab-eat-appl-fv 9-hunger 6-pumpkins
     'I eat pumpkins because of hunger.'

c.   Maúngú   ndí-ma-dy-él-á   njala.
     6-pumpkins 1st sing-hab-eat-appl-fv 9-hunger
     'Pumpkins I eat because of hunger.'

d.   Maûngu   ndí-ma-wa-dy-él-á   njala.
     6-pumpkins 1st sing-hab-6OM-eat-appl-fv 9-hunger
     'Pumpkins, I eat them because of hunger.'

e.   *Njala   ndí-ma-i-dy-él-á   maûngu.
     9-hunger 1st sing-hab-9OM-eat-appl-fv 6-pumpkins

It is this ability to introduce NPs that have a wide range of semantic roles that has contributed to the interest in studies of the applicative in Bantu languages and in their relevance to matters of theoretical interest (cf. Bokamba 1976, 1981; Bresnan and Moshi 1990; Mchombo 1993c).

5.15   Constraints on morpheme co-occurrence

The causative and the applicative can, and do in fact, co-occur. However, there is a restriction on the ordering of the two suffixes in Chichewa. While the suffixation of the applicative extension to a verb stem with a causative suffix is common, the immediate suffixation of a causative suffix to a verb stem with an applicative morpheme is rare. Consider the following:

(51) a.   Kalulú   a-ku-phík-íts-íl-a   mkángó maûngu
           1a-hare 1SM-pres-cook-caus-appl-fv 3-lion   6-pumpkins
           (kwá   chigawênga).
           (by   7-terrorist)
           'The hare is getting pumpkins cooked for the lion (by the terrorist).'

   b. *Kalulú   a-ku-phík-íl-íts-á   mkángó maûngu.
       *1a-hare   1SM-pres-cook-appl-caus-fv 3-lion   6-pumpkins

Issues pertaining to constraints on verb-stem morphotactics will be taken up in the next chapter. It should be noted that the ordering restriction of causative occurring before applicative, rather than the other way round, does not appear to be made necessary by semantic considerations. Verb-stem morphotactics in Bantu, and the principles that determine morpheme order and co-occurrence restrictions, constitute topics of on-going study (cf. Baker 1992; Hyman 1991, 2003; Hyman and Mchombo 1992; Sibanda 2004). We will postpone further discussion of this issue. This chapter has been mainly concerned with argument-structure-increasing processes, the causative, and the applicative (cf. Abasheikh 1978; Hoffman 1991; Mchombo 1978). In the next chapter we will turn attention to argument-structure-reducing processes. These include the passive, the stative, and the reciprocal of the extensions that are productive.

6

Argument-structure-reducing suffixes

6.1 Introductory remarks

This chapter will be devoted to a few extensions that have in common the property that they eliminate one NP from the range of required arguments within the clause structure. Each one of them has interesting theoretical issues surrounding it. These will be commented upon in the course of discussion of the phenomena, rather than taken up separately. Of the extensions that reduce the number of required arguments of the predicate, the passive is probably the best known and the most discussed. Its status within linguistic theory was enhanced by its involvement in the original formulations of the theory of transformational generative grammar (cf. Chomsky 1957). The observation was that selectional restrictions are preserved under passivization, as shown in the sentences below:

(1) a. John frightens sincerity.
    b. Sincerity is frightened by John.

Such preservation of selectional restrictions constituted part of the rationale for setting up underlying syntactic structures, where the selectional restrictions are specified. These are then mapped on to syntactic representations that receive phonological interpretation by grammatical transformations. The transformational rules, which could alter grammatical relations and yielded different surface structure representations, did not change the selectional restrictions. It was a short step from that to the claim that when properly formulated, transformational operations do not change meaning, a view that received its clearest formulation in the work of Katz and Postal (1964). It was incorporated into the detailed exposition of the theory of transformational generative grammar in Chomsky (1965) (cf. Hall Partee 1971; Jackendoff 1972). The passive was central to the formulation of various aspects of the theory of transformational generative grammar. Later, it was to play a crucial role in the articulation of lexicalist approaches to grammatical theory (Brame 1976; Bresnan 1978, 1982b; Mchombo 1978). Discussion of argument-structure-reducing morphology will begin with the passive extension.

6.2   The passive

The passive in Chichewa is easy to state. It is marked by the suffix -idw-
(and -edw-). It has the effect of "demoting" the subject NP to the status of an
oblique, marked as the object of the preposition ndí, while making the object NP
the subject. Consider the following:

(2) a.   Kalulú   a-ku-phík-á   maûngu.
          1a-hare 1SM-pres-cook-fv 6-pumpkins
          'The hare is cooking pumpkins.'

    b.   Maúngu   a-ku-phík-ídw-a   (ndí kálŭlu).
          6-pumpkins 6SM-pres-cook-pass-fv (by 1a-hare)
          'The pumpkins are being cooked (by the hare).'

The oblique NP can be omitted, as in English. The passive verb does not allow the
occurrence of the OM, as shown by the following:

(3)   *Maungu   a-ku-wa-phik-idw-a   ndí kálŭlu.
       *6-pumpkins 6SM-pres-6OM-cook-pass-fv by 1a-hare

In some respects this gives the overview of the passive in Chichewa. However,
there are cases when the passive morpheme appears attached to intransitive verbs.
When it does, it has the effect of marking the subject NP as lacking control of the
indicated activity. This is common with verbs that deal with bodily functions, such
as urinating, getting sexually aroused, etc. This is illustrated by the following:

(4)   kodz-a 'urinate'   kodz-édw-a 'involuntary urination'
       nyel-a 'defecate'   nyel-édw-a 'involuntary bowel movement'
       f-a 'die'   f-édw-a 'be in bereavement'
       uk-a 'wake up, rise'   uk-ídw-a 'be sexually aroused'

The passive interacts with causatives and applicatives subject to a number of
restrictions. For a start, the passive can apply to causative or applicative constructions, but the occurrence of the causative or applicative suffixes after the passive
suffix is not common, with minor exceptions. Thus, the following, in which there is
passive of a causative in (5a), and passive of an applicative in (5b), are grammatical:

(5) a.   Chigawênga chi-ku-phwány-íts-idw-á   maûngu   (ndí mkângo).
          7-terrorist   7SM-pres-smash-caus-pass-fv 6-pumpkins (by 3-lion)
          'The terrorist is made to smash pumpkins (by the lion).'

    b.   Mkángó u-na-phík-íl-idw-á   maûngu   (ndí kálŭlu).
          3-lion   3SM-pst-cook-appl-pass-fv 6-pumpkins (by 1a-hare)
          'The lion was cooked pumpkins (by the hare).'

The passive can apply to applicativized causatives as well (i.e. causative followed
by the applicative extension), as indicated by sentence (6) below:

(6)   Mkángó u-ku-phík-íts-il-idw-á   maûngu   (kwá chigawênga)
        3-lion   3SM-pres-cook-caus-appl-pass-fv 6-pumpkins (by   7-terrorist)
        (ndí kálŭlu).
        (by 1a-hare)
        'The lion is getting pumpkins cooked for it (by the terrorist) (at the instigation
        of the hare).'

Although the benefactive applicative can be passivized, other applicatives show
some restrictions. For instance, the patient NP *maûngu* in the benefactive applicative cannot become the subject of the passive. Comparable restrictions apply to
the instrumental applicative. The instrumental NP can be the subject of the passive of the instrumental applicative but the patient NP may not. The reason or
circumstantial applicative, on the other hand, is never passivizable. Consider the
following:

(7) a.   Kalulú a-ku-phík-íl-á   njala   maûngu
         1a-hare 1SM-pres-cook-appl-fv 9-hunger 6-pumpkins
         'The hare is cooking pumpkins because of hunger.'

    b.   *Njala   i-ku-phk-íl-ídw-a   maûngu   (ndí kálŭlu).
         *9-hunger 9SM-pres-cook-appl-pass-fv 6-pumpkins (by 1a-hare)

There are at least two cases where the applicative suffix may be attached to the
passive. These have to do with the locative and reason or circumstantial applicatives. This is illustrated by the following:

(8) a.   Maúngu   a-ku-phík-ídw-il-á   njala.
         6-pumpkins 6SM-pres-cook-pass-appl-fv 9-hunger
         'The pumpkins are being cooked for reasons of hunger.'

    b.   Maúngu   a-ku-phík-ídw-il-á   pa   chulu
         6-pumpkins 6SM-pres-cook-pass-appl-fv 16-on 7-anthill
         'The pumpkins are being cooked on the anthill.'

It is significant that the cases where the passive precedes the applicative involve
locative and circumstantial roles. These roles are low on the thematic hierarchy
and the passive verbs are subsumed to the class of unaccusatives. These facts seem
pertinent. For more detailed discussion of the relevance of the order of passive
before applicative, with a lexicalist analysis of the passive, see Alsina (1990).

6.3   Locative inversion and the passive

There is a class of intransitive verbs that involve optional specification of
the location. This is shown by the following sentence:

(9) a. Njovu   i-ná-gw-a   pa   chulu.
        9-elephant 9SM-pst-fall-fv 16-loc 7-anthill
        'An elephant fell on the anthill.'

The significant thing about such intransitive verbs is that they allow an alternative
construction in which the locative appears to be the subject, and the subject NP is
placed in the postverbal position. This is shown in sentence (9b) below:

    b. Pa   chulu   pa-ná-gw-á   njovu.
        16-loc 7-anthill 16SM pst fall-fv 9-elephant
        'On the anthill fell an elephant.'

(10) a. Njôka   y-a-gón-á   pa   mkéka.
         9-snake 9SM-perf-sleep-fv 16-loc 4-mat
         'A snake is sleeping on the mat.'

     b. Pa   mkéká pa-a-gon-á   njôka.
         16-loc 4-mat 16SM-perf-sleep-fv 9-snake
         'On the mat is sleeping a snake.'

There is a proverb in Chichewa that makes the claim that:

     c. M'chiuno   mw-á   mwána sí-mú-f-á   nkhúku.
         18-loc-7-waist 18SM-assoc 1-child neg-18SM-die-fv 9-chicken
         'Around the waist of a child a chicken does not die.' (= a child should not be
         pampered with gifts for performing well or overly praised for good conduct.
         The credit should go to the parents.)[1]

Such constructions are termed locative inversion. In detailed studies, it has been
shown that there are conditions on the types of verbs that allow locative inversion.
They are verbs whose sole argument is non-agentive. Specifically the NP must
have a patient or theme semantic role (Bresnan 1994; Bresnan and Kanerva 1989;
Bresnan and Zaenen 1990; Harford 1989). This property assimilates these verbs
to the class of unaccusative verbs. For verbs that are intransitive, but whose sole
argument does not have a patient role, locative inversion is ordinarily not possible.
Note the following:

(11) a. Atsíkáná a-ku-vín-á   mu   chipinda.
         2-girls   2SM-pres-dance-fv 18-loc 7-room
         'Girls are dancing in the room.'

     b. *Mu   chipinda mu-ku-vín-á   atsíkana.
          18-loc 7-room   18SM-pres-dance-fv 2-girls

---

[1] In some traditional dances, the best dancer is normally rewarded with a chicken. The
chicken represents an accolade best appreciated by an adult. This extends to ordinary life
in that recognition for children's achievements should be directed at the adults who raise
them.

Note that in Chichewa the locative does indeed appear to function as the subject in that the SM on the verb has the class features of the locative. On the other hand, the postverbal NP does not function as a typical grammatical object. For a start, it cannot have its features marked in the verbal morphology by an OM. This could also be a consequence of the fact that the verb is intransitive anyway, hence does not have an object. One thing that the postverbal subject acquires in that position is focus. The locative inversion construction is exploited for presentational focus (cf. Chimbutane 2002; Demuth 1990). The postverbal position appears to be a focus position. This is evident from the observation that in question formation in Bantu, the question words are normally placed in postverbal positions. Question formation is involved in focus construction (cf. Aboh 1999). The placement of the question words suggests that the postverbal position is a focus position. Consider the following example:

(12)   Chiombankhánga chí-ma-máng-á   bwánji zisa?
        7-eagle   7SM-hab-build-fv how   8-nests
        'How does an eagle build nests?'

In this, the question is about how the eagle 'builds nests.' Instead of the question word *bwánji* 'how' appearing after the entire verb phrase *chí-ma-mángá zisa* 'it builds nests,' it is placed immediately after the verb because it is the focus position. In locative inversion, the subject is thus placed in a focus position yielding what has been termed presentational focus (Demuth 1990; Harford 1989).

Returning to the passive and locative inversion, what is clear is that transitive verbs do not allow locative inversion.

(13) a.   Njovu   zi-ku-dy-á   maûngu   pa   chulu.
          10-elephants 10SM-pres-eat-fv 6-pumpkins 16-loc 7-anthill
          'Elephants are eating pumpkins on the anthill.'

     b.   *Pa   chulu   pa-ku-dy-á   njovu   maûngu.
          18-loc 7-anthill 18SM-pres-eat-fv 10-elephants 6-pumpkins

With transitive verbs, locative inversion is possible when the verb has been passivized.

(14) a.   Maúngu   a-ku-dy-édw-á   pa   chulu   (ndí njovu).
          6-pumpkins 6SM-pres-eat-pass-fv 16-loc 7-anthill (by 10-elephants)
          'Pumpkins are being eaten on the anthill (by elephants).'

     b.   Pa   chulu   pa-ku-dy-édw-á   maûngu.
          16-loc 7-anthill 16SM-pres-eat-pass-fv 6-pumpkins
          'On the anthill are being eaten pumpkins.'

This seems to argue for the assimilation of the passive verbs in Chichewa to the class of unaccusative verbs. It also demonstrates that the passive morpheme in Chichewa is indeed a detransitivizing affix. It is a morpheme that reduces the array of arguments of the predicate to which it applies. In the case of intransitive verbs that can take a passive morpheme, as in the examples in (4) above, they share with the rest of the passive constructions the requirement that the sole argument be non-agentive. It must be a patient or theme, something that lacks the power to control the event.

In some Bantu languages, such as Xhosa, the passive is also used in impersonal constructions (Dlayedwa 2002). Chichewa does not involve the passive in impersonal constructions that could not be assimilated to locative inversion.

6.4   The stative

The stative construction in Bantu languages involves the suffixation of the morpheme with the phonological shape of -k-, or -ik- and -ek-, to the verbal radical. The general condition on the suffixation of this morpheme is that the verb be transitive. It eliminates the subject NP, making it inexpressible in the syntactic structure, while converting the object NP of the input verb into the subject. Although the construction will be designated the stative, this being the most commonly used label, it should be indicated that the construction has also been identified by other labels. These have included such terms as neuter, neuter-passive, quasi-passive, neuter-stative, metastatic-potential, descriptive passive (see Satyo 1985). Such a proliferation of labels indicates uncertainty among Bantuists about how to characterize the process involved. The choice of the label "stative" is based on the observation that the verb denotes the result state of the base verb. In fact, some semantic restrictions, to be discussed later, do suggest something like this. It is also the label that is most widely used. The specific facts covered by this construction will be spelt out in detail.

The stative construction in Chichewa is derived through the suffixation of the -ik- morpheme to a transitive verb. The NP that was the object becomes the subject and the former subject is not expressible, not even as an oblique function. This is illustrated below:

(15) a.   Mbidzí   zi-na-pínd-á   maúta.
        10-zebra 10SM-pst-bend-fv 6-bows
        'The zebras bent the bows.'

     b.   Maúta   a-na-pind-ik-a   (*ndí mbǐdzi).
        6-bows 6SM-pst-bend-stat-fv (*by 10-zebras)
        'The bows got bent (*by the zebras).'

(16) a.   Akazitápé a-ku-ónóng-a   njínga.
        2-spies   2SM-pres-damage-fv 10-bicycles
        'The spies are damaging the bicycles.'

b. Njingá   zi-ku-ónóng-ĕk-a   (*ndí ákazitápe).
    10-bicycles 10SM-pres-damage-stat-fv (*by 2-spies)
    'The bicycles are getting damaged (*by the spies).'

The inability to have the subject of the transitive verb expressed marks the minimal difference between the stative construction and the passive, which it closely resembles. Thus, the passives of sentences (15a) and (16a) above, supplied below as (17a) and (17b) respectively, have the subject NP expressed as an oblique:

(17) a. Maútá   a-na-pínd-ídw-á   ndí mbídzi.
         6-bows 6SM-pst-bend-pass-fv by 10-zebras.
         'The bows were bent by the zebras.'

     b. Njingá   zi-ku-ónóng-edw-á   ndí ákazitápe.
         10-bicycles 10SM-pres-damage-pass-fv by 2-spies
         'The bicycles are being damaged by the spies.'

The stative cannot be suffixed to an intransitive verb, as the following data show:

(18)   nyow-a 'get wet' *nyow-ék-a
         gw-a   'fall'   *gw-ék-a
         lil-a   'cry'   *lil-ík-a
         ulúk-a 'fly'   *uluk-ík-a

The difference between the stative and the passive is not merely confined to the potential for expressing the subject of the transitive construction; there are differences that are more semantic in nature. The stative, unlike the passive, appears to have as part of its core meaning certain qualities or a state inherent to, or acquired through, its subject. It also seems to have the semantics of the subject's entering a particular state or condition, but such that there is no implication of agency responsible for such a state or condition (cf. Bokamba 1981; Guthrie 1962). Such attribution of qualities is exemplified by the following:[2]

(19) a. Maútá ó-pínd-ík-a
         6-bows 6assoc-bend-stat-fv
         'Bows that are bent (bent bows)'

     b. Njingá   zó-ónóng-ĕk-a
         10-bicycles 10assoc-damage-fv
         'Damaged bicycles'

The passive does not have comparable semantics. Although the two grammatical processes of passivization and stativization appear to derive from comparable sources, there are other strictly grammatical differences between them that demand explanation. These include the fact that not every transitive construction can be stativized, although passivization is not similarly constrained. To illustrate this,

---

[2] In Chichewa, the associative marker *á* and the infinitive marker *ku* fuse into *o* when the verb is not monosyllabic. So, for example, *á + ku-píndíka* becomes *ópíndíka*.

we will consider the cases that involve the causative and the applicative in their interaction with both the passive and the stative:

(20) a. Mbidzí   zi-ku-pínd-íts-a   kalulú máúta.
         10-zebras 10SM-pres-bend-caus-fv 1a-hare 6-bows
         'The zebras are making the hare bend the bows.'

   b. Kalúlú a-ku-pínd-íts-idw-á   máúta ndí mbǐdzi.
       1a-hare 1SM-pres-bend-caus-pass-fv 6-bows by 10-zebras
       'The hare is being made to bend bows by the zebras.'

   c. ?Kalulú wo-pínd-íts-ik-á   máúta.
       1a-hare 1assoc-bend-caus-stat-fv 6-bows

   d. Mautá   ó-pínd-íts-ǐk-a
       6-bows 6assoc-bend-caus-stat-fv
       'Bows that can be made bendable'

Sentence (20a) is readily passivizable, as shown in (20b). The stative, on the other hand, appears to have some restrictions. This situation is in sharp contrast with the case involving the applicative that introduces the benefactive. Consider the following:

(21) a. Mbidzí   zi-ku-pínd-íl-á   kalulú maúta.
         10-zebras 10SM-pres-bend-appl-fv 1a-hare 6-bows
         'The zebras are bending the bows for the hare.'

   b. Kalulú a-ku-pínd-íl-idw-á   maúta ndí mbǐdzi.
       1a-hare 1SM-pres-bend-appl-pass-fv 6-bows by 10-zebras
       'The hare is having the bows bent for him by the zebras.'

   c. *Kalulú wó-pínd-íl-ik-á   maúta
       1a-hare 1assoc-bend-appl-stat-fv 6-bows

   d. *Mautá   ó-pínd-íl-ǐk-a
       6-bows 6assoc-bend-appl-stat-fv

As the above examples show, while the attachment of the stative to the causative is possible, with some restrictions, the addition of the stative to the applicative is impossible. Note that the applicative is passivizable, as shown in (21b). Recall that the applicative in Chichewa introduces arguments into the syntactic structure with semantic roles that range over beneficiary, goal, instrument, location, and the circumstantial. The language does not permit the suffixation of the stative to an applicative irrespective of the argument role that the applicative is associated with. What principles account for these properties?

The restrictions that seem to apply to the stative do not seem to be motivated by considerations of the transitivity of the verb. The causative and the applicative are both transitive. The difference between the two has to do with the roles of the arguments involved, occasionally referred to as thematic roles. Apparently it is such thematic information associated with the verb semantics that seems to be relevant to the difference between the stative and the passive. Thematic structure is the aspect of verb semantics that is relevant to syntactic structure. In other words, it is the aspect of meaning that is accessible to syntactic rules or principles, just as the level of logical form (LF) within the theory of government and binding characterizes the contribution that grammar makes to meaning (cf. Chomsky 1985; May 1985). Let us pursue this issue a little further.

6.5   Approaches to the stative construction in Chichewa

The stative in Chichewa satisfies the standard requirements of a morpholexical operation. It is not merely correlated with specific morphology, but its presence affects the argument structure of the form to which it is suffixed. In virtually the entire tradition of Bantu linguistics the stative has been analyzed in terms of its similarities to, and difference from, the passive. This is not accidental in that the stative construction involves an intransitive construction whose subject NP is associated with the thematic role of patient/theme. In this respect the stative runs parallel to the passive construction whose sole argument may be a patient/theme. Both constructions result from morpholexical rules which eliminate one NP, normally an NP bearing the role of agent, and associate an NP bearing the role of patient/theme with the subject function. The affinity between these two processes is highlighted by Baker who observes that "it is well known that Passive functions cross-linguistically to make sentences less agentive and more stative" (Baker 1988a: 400). However, the two have some differences. The passive, but not the stative, allows the overt expression of the agent in a 'by-phrase'; the passive, but not the stative, allows for NPs other than those expressing the patient/theme to be associated with the subject. This is exemplified in part by example (21b) above, in which the benefactive is the subject, as well as by the following:

(22) a.   Alenje   a-ku-máng-íl-a   chingwe nkhúni.
           2-hunters   2SM-pres-tie-appl-fv   7-rope   10-firewood
           'The hunters are tying the firewood with the rope.'

     b.   Chingwe chi-ku-máng-íl-ídw-á   nkhúni   (ndí álenje).
           7-rope   7SM-pres-tie-appl-pass-fv   10-firewood (by 2-hunters)
           'The rope is being tied around the firewood (by the hunters).'

     c.   *Chingwe chi-ku-máng-íl-ik-á   nkhúni
           7-rope   7SM-pres-tie-appl-stat-fv   10-firewood

In this example, the subject of the passive is a nominal that has the role of instrument. These facts show that the stative and the passive are more different than they are similar. There is further evidence of this. The stative has the semantics of the inchoative that the passive lacks, and the absence of the agent in the stative is brought out syntactically in control constructions. The following examples show this difference:

(23) a.   Maútá   a-na-pínd-ídw-a   ku-ónétsa ku-khúmúdwa.
          6-bows 6SM-pst-bend-pass-fv   inf-show   inf-be disappointed
          'The bows were bent (in order) to show disappointment.'

   b.   *Maútá   a-na-pínd-ík-a   ku-ónétsa ku-khúmúdwa
          6-bows 6SM-pst-bend-stat-fv inf-show   inf-be disappointed

(24) a.   Mbidzí   zi-na-ph-édw-a   kutí pa-sa-khál-é   mkangano.
          10-zebras 10SM-pst-kill-pass-fv that 17on-neg-be-subjun 3-quarrel
          'The zebras were killed so that there shouldn't be (any) quarrels.'

   b.   *Mbidzí   zi-na-ph-ék-a   kutí pa-sa-khál-é   mkangano
          10-zebras 10SM-pst-kill-stat-fv that 17on-neg-be-subjun 3-quarrel

These examples show that the passive has an implicit controller argument which the stative lacks, a property that Chichewa shares with other Bantu languages. For instance, comparable facts seem to hold in Kikamba, a Bantu language spoken in Kenya. In that language the passive is marked by -*w*-, and the stative is realized by -*k*-. As Thomas-Ruzic has observed, "-*w*- on the verb indicates that the subject of the clause is non-agentive. Non-agentive subjects include patients, locatives, recipients, and benefactives, but they exclude instruments. The presence of -*w*- always implies the participation of an agent in the action. The agent itself, however, may or may not be expressed in the oblique" (Thomas-Ruzic 1990). Kikamba, unlike Chichewa, does not have an instrumental applicative, for comparison with regard to passivization. Given these observations, how is the stative to be analyzed in Chichewa, and other Bantu languages at that?

Regardless of the variations in proposals relating to morpholexical processes offered by competing theories, it is the case that the stative in Chichewa applies to an input configuration that is not just transitive, but has the thematic roles of agent and patient/theme. The result of its application is that the agent is eliminated and the patient/theme becomes the sole argument of the stative verb. The patient is then associated with the subject function. The requirement that at the point of its application the input configuration have an argument structure comprising agent and patient/theme roles accounts for the syntax of the stative in Chichewa. The passive differs from the stative in that it is not constrained by comparable conditions. In effect, the similarity between the two rests on the fact that the thematic configuration to which the stative applies is a proper subset of the configurations that can get passivized. In both cases the agent is eliminated. In the case of the stative, the agent must be eliminated altogether whereas in the passive it is merely suppressed, in other words, it remains syntactically active although it cannot be a target for other morpholexical rules. This accounts for its ability to be an implicit argument that can function as a controller.

In discussion of the passive and the stative in Chichewa, Dubinsky and Simango propose to capture the differences between the two differently. They hypothesize a level of lexical conceptual structure (cf. Jackendoff 1990) that is linked to the level of argument structure. The latter is then linked to grammatical functions for expression in the overt syntax. The elimination of the agent role in stative constructions is claimed to occur during the mapping of the lexical conceptual structure to the argument structure. The suppression of the agent role under passivization is a consequence of the fact that the passive applies to the level of mapping argument structure to grammatical functions or to overt structure. This is a crude summary of their analysis but it remains faithful to their overall view (cf. Bature 1991; Dubinsky and Simango 1996).

The claim that the syntax of the stative is insightfully handled in terms of the thematic role of its argument is further supported by investigations of the consequences of this analysis. Specifically, this analysis of the stative would suggest that the stative should be subsumed into the phenomenon of unaccusativity (Bresnan and Zaenen 1990; Perlmutter 1978).

6.6   On the unaccusativity of the stative in Chichewa

We have noted above that intransitive verbs subdivide into two, unaccusatives and unergatives, to use the terminology originally introduced by Perlmutter. The distinction is based on the syntactic or semantic properties of the argument. The sole argument of unaccusatives behaves like the object of the transitive verbs, while that of unergatives displays the characteristics of a basic subject. However, accounts of the unaccusative–unergative distinction in terms of the syntactic similarity of the subject with basic objects or subjects turn out to lack cross-linguistic generality. Instead, it has been noted that what distinguishes unaccusatives from the unergatives is best captured in terms of the thematic role associated with the subject NP. Unaccusatives have a patient/theme NP as the highest expressed role whereas unergatives have an agentive subject. This classification of the intransitive verbs seems to account for variable behavior that constructions involving them manifest with respect to a number of grammatical processes. For instance, in Italian, unaccusatives select the auxiliary *essere* while unergatives select *avere* and, further, unaccusatives but not unergatives allow *ne*-cliticization (cf. Torrego 1998). In English, the syntax of what are called resultatives seems to be handled in terms of the resultatives being predicated of an argument that is thematically patient (cf. Bresnan and Zaenen 1990; Goldberg 1992). For Chichewa, the phenomenon of locative inversion is intimately connected with the unaccusativity of the verb. It is only those constructions whose highest expressed role, normally appearing as the subject, has a patient/theme role that can undergo locative inversion (Bresnan and Kanerva 1989).

Taking this as characteristic of unaccusatives in Chichewa, it turns out that the stative fits in rather neatly with such verbs. This is demonstrated by its participation in locative inversion. Consider the following:

(25) a. Maútá   a-a-pind-ĭk-a   pa   chulu.
          6-bows 6SM-perf-bend-stat-fv 17-on 7-anthill
          'Bows have got bent on the anthill.'

     b. Pa   chulu   pa-a-pind-ik-á   maúta.
          17-on 7-anthill 17SM-perf-bend-stat-fv 6-bows
          'On the anthill bows have got bent.'

The locative inversion examples are significant in that they show that the stative does indeed behave like an unaccusative. This, once again, derives from the fact that the subject of the stative, as is the case with unaccusatives in general, bears the thematic role of patient. This means that the derivation of the statives in this language must be regulated by the presence of such thematic information. The requirement that the sole argument of the stative be a patient motivates a thematically based account of the interaction of the stative with other suffixes in Chichewa. This will be reviewed later, when attention will turn to constraints on morpheme order. Of relevance to current discussion is the interaction between the stative and the applicative.

It has been noted that the stative does not interact with the other suffixes as readily as the passive. For instance, statives of applicatives are not possible. Applicatives of the stative are possible but only when the applicative either introduces location, or is circumstantial (reason), or introduces what may be termed the maleficiary (cf. Harford 1993). This is the reading of something befalling someone. This is shown below:

(26) a. Maúngu   a-a-phwany-ik-il-á   pa   chulu.
          6-pumpkins 6SM-perf-smash-stat-appl-fv 16-on 7-anthill
          'The pumpkins have got smashed on the anthill.'

     b. Maúngu   a-a-phwany-ik-il-á   phúzo.
          6-pumpkins 6SM-perf-smash-stat-appl-fv 5-spite
          'The pumpkins have got smashed out of spite.'

     c. Maúngu   a-a-chí-phwány-ík-ĭl-a   (chigawênga).
          6-pumpkins 6SM-perf-7OM-smash-stat-appl-fv (7-terrorist)
          'The pumpkins have got smashed on him (the terrorist).'

Perhaps because the malefactive reading requires an animate entity, the malefactive applicative normally requires the inclusion of the OM, as in (26c) above. The fact that the malefactive applicative can apply to a stative verb while the benefactive applicative does not seems to suggest that the two are different. This is a vexed issue since some researchers have argued that the two are not that different (cf. Harford 1991). Note that the malefactive reading was also the one attributed to the possessor-raising construction discussed earlier (chapter 5). For those who might entertain the idea of separating the beneficiary from the maleficiary, one approach to dealing with this is to set up a hierarchy of thematic roles. The roles that the applicative can introduce into a configuration with a stative could be claimed to rank lower than the patient/theme role, the sole argument of the stative. It is an open question whether thematic roles constitute a hierarchy and thematic role information is relevant to statement of morpheme order. We will examine this issue below. First, attention will be turned to the other argument-structure-reducing process, the reciprocal.

6.7   The reciprocal

It would be expected of a section that purports to discuss the reciprocal that it would also deal with the reflexive. Indeed the separation of the reciprocal from the reflexive, with separate accounts of each, might look contrived or artificial. The two have been treated together under the theory of bound anaphora in recent work in grammatical theory. The inclusion of the reciprocal in discussion of argument-structure-changing morphology is justifiable but the exclusion of the reflexive seems suspicious. This is because there are studies of Bantu languages in which reflexivization has been claimed to be an argument-structure-reducing process. This view is adopted for Tsonga by Matsinhe, exploiting ideas from Grimshaw (cf. Matsinhe 1994). What then is the rationale for keeping them separate?

The obvious difference between the reflexive and the reciprocal in Bantu is in their distribution. The reciprocal in Chichewa, and in most Bantu languages, is marked by the suffix -an-. The verb appears with one NP, in the plural. This is achieved either by having a subject NP that denotes a group or by having a co-ordinate structure in the subject position. Note the following:

(27) a.   Mikángó i-ku-phwány-an-a.
          4-lions   4SM-pres-smash-recip-fv
          'Lions are smashing one another.'

    b.   Mbûzi   ndí nkhôsa   zi-ku-mény-an-a.
          10-goats and 10-sheep 10SM-pres-hit-recip-fv
          'Goats and sheep are hitting each other.'

The cases involving co-ordinate NPs normally introduce some problems because of the noun classification system that is characteristic of Bantu languages. In brief, the co-ordinate NP structure in the subject position must have an appropriate subject marker. A comparable problem arises when there is a co-ordinate structure with a topic function to which an OM has to be linked through anaphoric binding. In the examples given above, the problem has been minimized in that the co-ordinated nouns have been taken from the same class. Problems arise when the nouns come from different gender classes with different number features and there is no simple strategy by which a unique SM for the co-ordinate structure may be determined (cf. Corbett and Mtenje 1987; Marten 1999; Reynolds and Eastman 1989; Mchombo and Ngunga 1994). In that case the strategy appealed to is that of "extraposing" all but the first conjunct, which then determines the shape of the SM. This yields some version of a comitative construction. Consider the following:

(28) a. Mkángó ndí kálúlu ?-ku-páts-án-á   mphâtso.
         3-lion   and 1a-hare ?-pres-give-recip-fv 10-gifts
         'The lion and the hare are giving each other gifts.'

     b. Mkálgó u-ku-páts-án-a   mphâtso ndí kálúlu.
         3-lion   3SM-pres-give-recip-fv 10-gifts with 1a-hare
         'The lion and the hare are giving each other gifts.'

In many Bantu languages reflexivization is marked by an invariant morpheme which is prefixed to the VR in the slot marked OM, replacing the object marker. The reflexive morpheme is -*dzi*- in Chichewa, -*ji*- in Swahili, and -*zi*- in Xhosa. These are illustrated by the sentences (29a–c) below:

(29) a. Mkángó u-na-dzí-súpǔl-a.
         3-lion   3SM-pst-reflex-bruise-fv
         'The lion bruised itself.'

     b. Mvuvi   a-li-ji-kat-a.
         1-fisherman 1SM-pst-reflex-cut-fv
         'The fisherman cut himself.'

     c. Umntwana u-ya-zi-hlamb-a.
         1-child   1SM-pres-reflex-wash-fv
         'The child washes himself.'

Evidence that the reflexive morpheme is in the same structural position as the OM is offered by such Chichewa sentences as (30) below. In these, the ungrammaticality is induced by the co-occurrence of the reflexive and an OM:

(30) a. *Mkángó u-na-dzí-wá-páts-a   alenje.
          3-lion   3SM-pst-reflex-2OM-give-fv 2-hunters
          'The lion gave itself (them) the hunters.'

     b. *Mkángó u-na-wa-dzi-pats-a   alenje.
          3-lion   3SM-pst-2OM-reflex-give-fv 2-hunters
          'The lion gave itself to (them) the hunters.'

The difference in distribution appears to correlate with an array of other factors. Thus, the reciprocal is subject to all the processes that target the VS. These include the phonological process of vowel harmony, in those languages where it is attested, the morphological process of reduplication, nominalization, as well as in bare-stem imperatives. On the other hand, the reflexive is a clitic, suggesting that it is a syntactically independent but phonologically bound element. Like the OM, it fails to participate in the processes that apply to the VS. It is, in effect, an incorporated pronominal argument that is subject to the principles of bound anaphora. As such, it is not an argument-structure-changing morpheme. Naturally, this analysis of the reflexive requires further comment.

In his analysis of verbal affixes in Tsonga, a language spoken in Mozambique and South Africa, Matsinhe (1994) treats the reciprocal and the reflexive as having comparable effects. The reciprocal morpheme is -an-, as in Chichewa and in Bantu in general. According to Matsinhe, "this affix changes the predicate argument structure of the verb to which it is attached by binding the object (theme) to the subject (agent), creating coreferentiality. This fact makes the reciprocal affix -an- resemble the reflexive prefix -ti. Thus, the former will be treated on par with the latter" (1994: 169). The parity of treatment of the reflexive and the reciprocal is motivated by the observation that "[L]ike the reciprocal affix -an-, the reflexive prefix -ti- gives rise to coreferentiality between the agent and the theme. The theta role linked to the object is suppressed (bound to the subject), and, as a result, the number of the arguments is reduced by one" (1994: 170). Matsinhe adopts a suggestion by Grimshaw (1982) that "reflexivization should be regarded as a morpholexical operation which applies a reflexive lexical rule to the predi-cate argument structure of a verb, and whose effect is to bind one argument to another" (Grimshaw 1982:106). On the basis of that, Matsinhe makes the claim that reflexivization affects transitivity patterns, and that "given a transitive two-place predicate, a reflexive predicate can be derived from it by binding its object to the subject. Hence reflexivization can be regarded as a process which transforms a transitive verb into an intransitive one" (1994: 170).

This analysis of the reflexive, while plausible, is not necessarily compelling. For a start, it relies rather heavily on shifting conceptions of the notion of binding. In general, anaphoric binding deals with the resolution of referential dependencies of pronominal elements. In Bantu languages, the OMs have been analyzed as incorporated pronominal arguments that are bound to an antecedent outside the minimal clause. In Gikuyu, the OM is in complementary distribution with the object NP, as noted above (cf. Bergvall 1985; Mugane 1997). Yet, it is not claimed that the OM detransitivizes the verb, explaining thereby the omission of the object NP. The pronominal argument status of the OM is accepted, supported in part by its grammaticalization as a verbal prefix or clitic. As Allan (1983) states about Swahili, "a Swahili verb may take a cliticized object prefix" (Allan 1983: 323). The grammaticalization of the reflexive which, unlike the reciprocal, appears in the OM position, is somehow discounted as irrelevant to the determination of its status as a pronominal argument that is bound to an antecedent within the clause. Instead, the failure of the verb to support an object NP, comparable to the situation when the OM is present anyway, is construed as evidence that the reflexive is a detransitivizing affix. Note that in languages such as Chichewa which, unlike Gikuyu, allows for clitic doubling, i.e. for the putative object NP to co-occur with the OM, the said object NP is a Topic, anaphorically bound to the OM. The variable treatment of elements with comparable grammaticalization, whose complementarity reduces to the domains within which their referential values have to be resolved, that is, the domains of binding, is what requires explanation. This is not to deny that the reflexive is indeed a derivational morpheme in other languages, and may need to be treated alongside the reciprocal. In those languages where the reflexive and the reciprocal are in fact homophonous and share distributional properties, the case for unified treatment of the two is, indeed, compelling. The contention here is that the case for it as such in Chichewa and, possibly, other Bantu languages, has not been resolved, and the analysis of the reflexive as an anaphoric argument remains motivated. A plausible treatment of the reflexive in Bantu as a detransitivizing morpheme is one that might have to extend the privilege to the OM. Treatment of bound anaphora as an aspect of word induction, not as a relation between NPs, would provide the most plausible analysis of the reflexive and much else as non-argumental (cf. Brame 1983, 1984).

Further, note that the concept of binding that applies to the reciprocal is not entirely comparable to that applying to the reflexive. With the reflexive it is indeed true, as pointed out by Matsinhe, among others, that the reflexive prefix, -*ti*- in Tsonga, or -*dzi*- in Chichewa, gives rise to coreferentiality between the agent and the theme. The theta role linked to the object is suppressed (bound to the subject), and, as a result, the number of the arguments is reduced by one. This is because in reflexive constructions, the agent and the patient are identical. Thus, the subject and the object in the syntactic structure map on to the same entity in the conceptual domain (cf. Sells, Zaenen, and Zec 1987). The grammaticalization strategy may indeed exploit the detransitivization of the verb or the relation of binding. In reciprocal constructions, on the other hand, the verb is reduced to expressing a relation such that, in the simplest case, the agent and the patient stand in that relation to one another. Thus, the reciprocal captures the situation where given the relation R expressed by the reciprocal verb, R applies such that, of two individuals or entities x and y, Rxy and Ryx is true. The situation does quickly get complex when cardinality of the individuals increases and lexical aspects of the predicate are taken into consideration. In some cases, the reading yielded is simply that of group activity. Thus, consider the situation of a bar-room brawl, with a large number of individuals. The statement that the people threw bottles at each other does not mean that the relation of 'throwing bottles' holds of every pair-wise combination of the people there. Consider, further, the interpretation given to claims that animals followed each other to the river, for example, or that the substitute players in a sporting event are sitting next to each other on a bench. The interpretations are not comparable to that of, say, two individuals shouting insults at each other. The notion of binding as applied to the reciprocal is thus somewhat different from that of the reflexive (cf. Alsina 1993; Dalrymple et al. 1994, 1998; Mchombo 1999b, 2002a, b).

There are also semantic differences between the two. The noted asymmetric distribution, besides correlating with differences in behavior *vis-à-vis* a number of significant linguistic processes some of which have been enumerated above, seems to account for semantic differences between the two processes. One such semantic difference between the reflexive and the reciprocal revolves around bound variable interpretation or sloppy identity (cf. Bach, Bresnan, and Wasow 1974; Reinhart 1983; Sells, Zaenen, and Zec 1987). The following will illustrate the point:

(31) a. Alenje   á-ma-dzi-nyóz-á   ku-pósá   asodzi.
         2-hunters 2SM-hab-reflex-despise-fv inf-exceed 2-fishermen
         'The hunters despise themselves more than the fishermen.'

     b. Alenje   á-ma-nyoz-án-á   ku-pósá   asodzi.
         2-hunters 2SM-hab-despise-recip-fv inf-exceed 2-fishermen
         'The hunters despise each other more than the fishermen.'

Sentence (31b) is unambiguous, admitting only the interpretation that the hunters despise each other more than the fishermen despise each other. This is standard sloppy identity reading. On the other hand, the reflexive sentence in (31a) is ambiguous, allowing the following interpretations:

a. the hunters despise themselves more than the fishermen despise them
b. the hunters despise themselves more than they despise the fishermen
c. the hunters despise themselves more than the fishermen despise themselves
    (sloppy identity reading).

This difference in interpretation possibilities is explained if it is assumed that the reflexive, unlike the reciprocal, is a syntactic argument that functions as the object of the verb. As the reflexive is an object, by hypothesis the verb to which it is attached is transitive, i.e. is a predicate with two arguments. When a transitive verb is used in a comparative construction and only one argument is used in the second part of the comparison, the argument can be either the subject or the object of the transitive verb. This underlies the strict, non-sloppy readings, associated with the comparative construction involving the reflexive. This lends further support to the analysis of the reflexive and, *a fortiori*, the object markers in general, as pronominal. The reflexive, as an anaphor, is syntactically bound to the subject.

The reciprocal is different in that, for a start, it is not a syntactic argument. It is an aspect of the morphology that reduces by one the number of expressible arguments of the predicate. Admittedly, with regard to interaction with other morpholexical processes, such as passivization, or object marking, the reflexive and the reciprocal behave somewhat similarly. Take sentence (28b) above. Note that it cannot be passivized.

(32)   *Mphâtso i-ku-páts-án-ídw-á   ndí mkángo ndí kálúlu.
        9-gift   1SM-pres-give-recip-pass-fv with 3-lion   by 1a-hare

Neither can a reciprocalized verb take the OM, which always bears the function of the direct object. This is shown in the following:

(33)   *Mkángó u-ku-í-páts-án-á   ndí kálúlu (mphâtso)
        3-lion   3SM-pres-9OM-give-recip-fv with 1a-hare (9-gift)

In brief, the reciprocal fails the simplest diagnostics of transitive verbs. Does that imply that the reflexive verb has also been detransitivized? Note that the failure to have another OM can easily be attributed to the fact that Chichewa is not a multiple-object-marking language like Kichagga or Ki-Haya. Since the reflexive already occupies the OM, no other OM is allowed. With regard to passivization, the issue is not peculiar to Chichewa or Bantu. Languages such as English, where the reflexive is in an argument position, still resist the passivization of a sentence with the reflexive. The restriction may be attributed to violation of command relations necessary for binding. In brief, the question of whether the reflexive and the reciprocal are to be treated comparably as detransitivizing morphemes in Bantu remains somewhat open.

There is one area where the reciprocal and the reflexive are treated differently, and this is in manner nominalization. This topic will be dealt with in chapter 7.

Focusing more on the reciprocal, in its interaction with other suffixes the reciprocal does not co-occur with the stative, or with the passive unless there is the intervention of transitivizing affixes such as the applicative or the causative:

(34)   Anyání   a-na-mény-éts-án-ídw-á   ndí mikângo.
        2-baboons 2SM-pst-hit-caus-recip-pass-fv by 4-lions
        'The baboons were made to hit each other by the lions.'

In its co-occurrence with the applicative (as with the causative in other languages), the reciprocal is constrained to appear after the applicative suffix, irrespective of the nature of the applicative argument. There are examples such as the following:

(35)   Mikângo í-ma-tung-il-án-á   mădzi.
        4-lions   4SM-hab-draw-appl-recip-fv 6-water
        'Lions draw water for each other.'

In this example, the applicative is attached before the reciprocal and this correlates with semantic compositionality. However, note the following:

(36)   *Mikango i-ma-meny-an-il-a   pa   chulu.
        *4-lions   4SM-hab-hit-recip-appl-fv 16-on 7-anthill

Although this sentence is predicted to occur on the basis of semantic compositionality, it is ungrammatical. Semantic compositionality predicts it because the applicative introduces the location where the lions hit each other or fight. Thus, the reciprocal needs to be suffixed first to derive the reading of 'fight.' The applicative can then be suffixed to introduce the location. The sentence is ungrammatical because, for some reason, the reciprocal cannot precede the applicative. In order to meet the ordering constraints, either the applicative–reciprocal order is used, as in (37a and b), or, as in the case of the locative applicative, the reciprocal may need to be repeated after the applicative, as in (37c).

(37) a.   Anyaní   a-na-téng-él-án-á   zi-péso.
           2-baboons 2SM-past-take-appl-recip-fv 8-combs
           'Baboons brought (for) each other combs.'

     b.   Anyaní   a-na-téng-él-án-á   ku   dziwe.
           2-baboons 2SM-past-take-appl-recip-fv 17-loc 5-pool
           'Baboons took each other to the pool.'

     c.   Mikângo í-ma-meny-an-il-án-á   pa   chulu.
           4-lions 4SM-hab-hit-recip-appl-recip-fv 16-on 7-anthill
           'Lions hit each other on an anthill.'

The situation even holds in cases where the introduction of the applicative extension is not connected to argument structure. It was noted above (see chapter 4) that the relative marker -méne combines with class 18 locative marker mu, to yield a reading of non-interrogative 'how.' This is exemplified in sentences such as 'this is how baboons build huts.' In such constrcutions, the verb has to have the applicative extension, completely demanded by the presence of mméne 'how.' When the verb involves a reciprocal extension, the order is still required to be that of the applicative before the reciprocal, even when the syntactic motivation of the applicative extension would demand that it appear after the reciprocal. Thus, one gets examples such as the one provided in (37d) below, from textual material:

     d.   . . . ndi-ka-kumbukira   m-mene   ndi-na-dziw-ir-an-a
           . . . 1st pers-cond-remember 18SM-relpro 1st pers-pst-know-appl-recip-fv
           ndi   msungwana-yo, . . .
           with 1-girl-that
           'When I remember how that girl and I got to know each other . . .' (Zingani, 1989: 7)

In fact, the first chapter of Zingani's novelette carries the headline of *Mmene Tinapezerana* 'How We Found Each Other (Met).' Here, the verb is *péz-a* 'find.' To this the reciprocal is added to yield *péz-án-a* 'find each other.' The topic of the chapter is how that came about. However, instead of the applicative being affixed to the reciprocalized verb, it is affixed to the verb root, with the reciprocal affixed to it. This seems to point to a specific constraint, practically templatic, on the co-occurrence relations between the applicative and the reciprocal.

Thus, verb-stem morphotactics seem to derive partly from syntactic/semantic considerations, where these may crucially involve thematic information, and partly from purely morphological factors which, at this stage, are not very well understood (for some discussion, see Hyman 2003; Hyman and Katamba 1993; Hyman and Mchombo 1992; Mathangwane 1994; Ngunga 2000; Sibanda 2004). This issue will be revisited in the next chapter.

Besides its distribution and its interaction with other morphemes affecting argument structure, the reciprocal derives reciprocal verbs that lack an argument that participates in binding. This remains a major difference between the reciprocal and the reflexive. Whereas the reflexive is a syntactic argument that is anaphoric in nature, hence has to be bound by an antecedent within an appropriately characterized local domain, the reciprocal is a morpholexical operation that derives predicates with an argument structure different from that of the base predicate. In fact, it has been customary to include reciprocals in discussions of "symmetric predicates" in linguistics (cf. Lakoff and Peters 1966; McNally 1993). A two-place predicate, R, is said to be symmetric if for any two x and y, appropriate arguments of R, the following holds: Rxy is equivalent to Ryx. In other words, if "x is in the relation R to y, but y is not in the relation R to x" is contradictory, then R is said to be symmetric. It should be noted that this characterization of symmetric predicates does not include the resolution of referential dependency between two arguments. Rather, the focus is on the intrinsic properties of the relation itself. Any relation P for which Pxy = Pyx does not hold, for some suitable arguments x and y, is simply not symmetric (for detailed discussion see Dalrymple et al. 1994; Dalrymple, Mchombo, and Peters 1994; Mchombo 1992, 1999b; Mchombo and Ngalande 1980). In Chichewa the reciprocal morpheme, sometimes fossilized, is regularly present in symmetric predicates. Consider the following:

(38)   komana   'meet'
        sonkhana   'gather'
        pangana   'promise'
        kangana   'quarrel'
        bana   'elope' (lit., 'steal one other')

This attests to the intimate connection existing between reciprocals and symmetric predicates. The predicate status of the reciprocal is further brought out by the distributional properties that have been chronicled above. The reflexive, on the other hand, being a syntactic argument, is excluded from the domain of lexical operations or processes affecting argument structure but participates in the syntactic process of binding. This is a strategy by which referential dependencies are resolved in linguistic expressions.

6.8   The reversive and other unproductive affixes

According to Guthrie (1962) there are three types of extensions:

(i)   those that increase the number of expressible arguments by one, such as the causative and the applicative;

(ii)   those that reduce the number of expressible arguments by one, such as the passive, stative, and reciprocal;

(iii)   those that are neutral. These affect the meaning of the predicate but not the number of arguments. Of this last group the best known is the reversive.

The reversive is a common suffix that does not affect the number of the arguments that the derived verb takes. In Chichewa this is signaled by the suffix *-ul-*, as shown in the following:

(39)   tsek-a   'shut'   tsek-ul-a/tsegul-a 'open'
         v-al-a   'dress up'   v-ul-a   'undress'
         yal-a   'spread'   yal-ul-a   'unspread'
         mat-a   'stick'   mat-ul-a   'unglue'
         mang-a 'tie up'   mas-ul-a   'untie'

Typical examples of the reversive construction are shown below:

(40) a.   Anyání   a-ku-tsék-á   zenêla.
            2-baboons 2SM-pres-shut 5-window
            'The baboons are shutting the window.'

     b.   Anyání   a-ku-tsék-úl-a   zenêla.
            2-baboons 2SM-pres-shut-rev-fv 5-window
            'The baboons are opening the window.'

This suffix is no longer productive and it only appears with a small set of verbs. In other words, it is not freely affixed to other verbs. For instance, there is the verb *kwel-a* 'climb up' whose antonym is not **kwel-ul-a,* but *tsik-a* 'come down, descend.' There are even cases where it is conceivable that the *-ul-* that appears in them may have originally had to do with 'undoing' but where that aspect is no longer evident because the base form no longer exists. These are suggested by words such as *gwed-ul-a* 'dismantle, e.g. a chair,' or *gum-ul-a* 'demolish, e.g. a building.' There are no verbs *gwed-a* or *gum-a*.

There are other forms that may have originated as verbal suffixes, e.g.-*am*-, found in some verbs which denote something about body posture or position, but which are completely unproductive in Chichewa and only appear in frozen forms. Indeed the -*am*- suffix, sometimes referred to as the "positional extension," is found commonly in Bantu languages with a fixed set of verbal radicals that denote posture or body position. Chichewa affords a few verbs including the following: *wel-am-a* 'bend,' *pol-am-a* 'stoop,' *gad-am-a* 'lie on one's back,' *yand-am-a* 'float,' *pend-am-a* 'lean,' *l-am-a* 'survive,' *z-ám-a* 'get stuck, e.g. a car in mud.' This last one is tonally different from the rest, a fact that may be of some significance. There are cases where the notion of posture may be relatively abstract. Thus, there is the word *chat-am-a* 'keep quiet/shut up' that seems to be tenuously linked to this group. It probably has to do with the posture of the articulatory organs; and the word *lung-am-a* 'be just,' which has to do with mental disposition rather than physical body posture. The -*am*- suffix, labeled the "stative" in past work on Bantu linguistics (cf. Dembetembe 1987; Meeussen 1971) is neither isolable nor is it productively attached to other verb stems in Chichewa.

6.9   Conclusion

Argument-structure-reducing morphology has been the focus of attention in this chapter. These affixes constitute a significant subgroup of the verb-stem morphology. In some languages, e.g. Lunda, it has been observed that some verb-stem extensions have been lost, their function being taken over by impersonal constructions. Significantly, it is the set of argument-structure-reducing affixes that has been lost (cf. Kawasha 1999b). Coincidentally, in Xhosa, the passive is used in impersonal constructions too. It is conceivable that such constructions exploit these affixes but not the argument-structure-increasing ones. It would be expected that such clustering of properties would correlate with significant linguistic processes. Certainly the argument-structure-increasing morphemes are involved in double-object constructions. It is not clear whether the difference plays a role in constraining the order of morphemes within the verb stem. The verb stem is definitely the domain of significant linguistic processes, hence there could be principles of morpheme ordering that are operative in this domain but that do not operate outside it. In the next and final chapter, we will take note of some of the processes that target the verb stem.

7

The verb stem as a domain of linguistic processes

7.1   Introduction

The verb stem in Chichewa and Bantu languages in general has been determined to be the locus of significant linguistic processes. Some of these have been commented upon in the preceding chapters. This attests to the unique status it has in Bantu linguistic structure and to its lexical integrity. For instance, it has been pointed out that in those Bantu languages where vowel harmony is evident, it operates within the domain of the verb stem. In Chichewa the tones behave differently within the verb stem from outside that domain. It has been argued that the extensions are categorially verbal (cf. Mchombo 1999a).

The verb stem is the realization of what has been termed predicate composition (cf. Alsina 1993). Thus argument-structure changing can be cast in terms of predicate composition with attendant alteration of the array of arguments. In this chapter we will turn attention to some of the processes that target the verb stem, thus highlighting its integrity. The processes will include reduplication, nominalization, and, to the extent possible, principles that regulate the ordering of morphemes within it.

7.2   Reduplication

In Chichewa the verb stem is the part of the verb unit that gets reduplicated (cf. Mchombo 1993b; Mtenje 1988). None of the verbal prefixes participates in this process. Thus given an expression such as:

(1) a.   Anyání   á-ma-mang-its-il-án-á   zisakasa kwá míkângo.
         2-baboons 2SM-hab-build-caus-appl-recip-fv 8-huts   by   4-lions
         'The baboons get huts built for each other by (at the hands of) the lions.'

one gets the following reduplicated version to capture the idea of frequent or repeated activity:

    b.   Anyání á-ma-[mang-its-il-án-á]-[mang-its-il-án-á] zisakasa kwá míkângo.
         'The baboons frequently get huts built for each other by the lions.'

The reduplication of the verb stem offers some evidence of the integrity of that unit and suggests the presence of a more refined structure to the verbal morphology. The reduplication of the verb differs from that of nouns in that in the latter it applies to a prosodic structure. In Chichewa noun reduplication affects only the last two syllables or the final foot of the noun (see Kanerva 1990 for more details). This is shown in the following:

(2)   mwamûna 'man, male'   mwamúnámŭna 'real (macho) man'
         m-kâzi   'woman, female' mkázíkăzi   'cute and cultured woman'
         mu-nthu 'person'   munthumúnthu 'a real (humane) person'

In the case of the verb, the VR and the suffixes constitute a prosodic unit which is also a grammatical entity and is the domain of a number of linguistic processes. Besides reduplication it is the domain of vowel harmony (cf. Kanerva 1990; Mtenje 1985), as noted above. It is also the domain of derivation, as argued in the previous chapters (but see also Mchombo 1978), and, further, the verb stem is the input to nominalization processes, as shown below. In many respects, derivational morphology in Chichewa is primarily suffixing, while inflectional morphology is normally prefixal, and this holds, by and large, for nouns as well. The verb stem is the unit that is the sister constituent to the OM, with which it forms a higher unit, referred to as the *macrostem* or *suprastem* (Goldsmith and Sabimana 1985). The other prefixes are added to the macrostem to form the larger construction. The prefixes to the verb stem have been analyzed here as comprising clitics to the extent that this is not mere terminological preference, fitting into the category of inflectional morphemes. This makes the domain outside the VS that of inflectional morphology.

Reduplication itself has been argued to be a morphological process (cf. Levin 1983; Marantz 1982; Mtenje 1988). In Chichewa verbal reduplication the verb stem is the unit affected, attesting to its status as a morphological unit. In some Bantu languages, e.g. Kinande, there is partial reduplication. In such cases, sometimes it is the verb root that undergoes reduplication (see Mutaka and Hyman 1990), itself a significant morphological unit.

7.3   Nominal derivation

The process of nominal derivation in Chichewa takes the verb stem as input. The specific nominals under review here are those derived through the replacement of the final vowel [a] by either [i] for actor (agentive) nouns, or [o] for non-actor nominals. An appropriate gender-class prefix is then added to the noun stem to obtain the noun. Consider the following examples:

(3)   phunzíts-a   'teach'   m-phunzits-i   'teacher'
       sangalats-a   'amuse'   m-sangalats-i   'entertainer'
       lemb-a   'write'   m-lémbi   'secretary'
       lemb-a   'write'   chi-lémb-o   'script'
       tsek-a   'shut'   chi-tsek-o   'door'

Evidence for the claim that such nominalization takes the verb stem, i.e. verb roots that may have been extended by the extensions, derives from observations such as the following:

(4)   kónd-a   'love'   kónd-án-a   'love each other'   chi-kond-an-o   'mutual love'
       d-a   'hate'   d-an-a   'hate each other'   m-d-án-i   'enemy'
       kodz-a   'urinate'   kodz-el-a   'urinate with/at'   chi-kodz-el-o   'bladder'
       fun-a   'want'   fun-il-a   'wish for'   chi-fun-il-o   'desire'
       ongol-a   'straighten' ongol-el-a   'straighten with'   chiongol-el-o   'steering wheel'

The verb *tum-a* 'send (a person on an errand)' offers the nominals *mtumw-i* 'apostle, messenger.' As noted by Mtenje (p.c.) "[N]thumwi is a delegate and Mtumwi is someone sent on a religious mission (to preach the way of God) (both from the semantic root of *ku-túma* 'to send'). And indeed Mtumwi is biblical and one rarely hears this word these days except during sermons when reference is being made to the apostles." In effect *nthumwi* 'delegate(s)' seems to derive from this through desyllabification of the class 1 prefix. These nouns have the passive morpheme *-w-*, not productively used in Chichewa but still extant in such words as *kwatil-a* 'marry (of a man)' and *kwatiw-a* 'be married (of a woman).' The nominalization in the examples above involves a passivized verb.

The prefixes ordinarily add information concerning number and gender class, making them clearly inflectional. However, there are cases where they seem to straddle the border between inflection and derivation. That is to say, there are instances where the prefixes appear to be derivational. Consider the following:

(5)   kodz-a 'urinate'   m-kódz-o 'urine'   li-kódz-o 'bilharzia'
       lemb-a 'write'   m-lémbo 'handwriting'   chi-lémb-o 'script'
       lang-a 'advise, punish'   ma-lang-o 'advice'   chi-lang-o 'punishment'

This is even more robust with the verb *yend-a* 'walk, move,' from which the following nouns are derived using the noun-class prefixes:

       yenda 'walk, move' mlĕndo   'visitor, guest' u-lĕndo   'journey'
                          mwendo   'leg'   chi-lĕndo 'foreign, strange'

In these cases, the nominalizing suffix does not determine the full meaning of the noun, that being fixed by the class prefix. The role of the prefix in deriving words is even more clear in the derivation of abstract nouns. Consider the following adjective stems: *wísi* 'unripe,' *kúlu* 'big,' *módzi* 'one,' *káli* 'fierce.' From these the following abstract nouns are obtained through the prefixation of the class 14 marker *u-*. This yields such forms as *u-wísi* 'unripeness,' *u-kúlu* 'magnitude,' *u-módzi* 'unity,' *u-káli* 'ferocity.' These raise questions concerning the delimitation of inflectional from derivational morphology. Anderson discusses the derivational status of noun-class prefixes in Fula and relevant considerations are noted in Swahili by Reynolds and Eastman (Anderson 1985; Reynolds and Eastman 1989). Naturally, this serves to highlight, yet again, the perennial problem of the demarcation or delimitation of inflectional from derivational morphology.

In addition to that, there is also "manner nominalization" in Chichewa. This involves the suffixation of *-idwe* or *-edwe* to the verb stem, subject to vowel harmony, and the prefixation of *ka-* or *ma-* to the result. The reading of the output is that of 'the manner of V-ing.' This is illustrated by the following:

(6)   gumul-a   'demolish' ka-gumul-idwe   'the manner of demolishing'
       yendets-a 'drive'   ka-yendets-edw-e 'the manner of driving'
       lim-a   'cultivate' ma-lim-idwe   'the manner of cultivating'

The nouns that have the *ka-* prefix use the same prefix as the subject marker. Although this prefix is formally identical to that of class 12 for the diminutives, it is distinct from it. Those that have the *ma-* prefix pattern like class 6 nouns in that they have *a* as the subject marker. Although the *ma-* prefix is not a pluralizer, a function it has when it marks class 6 nouns, for agreement patterns derived nominals are treated as if they belong to that class. By parity of reasoning, the nominals with *ka-* will be marked as class 12 since they use a form that is identical to that of class 12. This is shown in the following:

(7)   Ka-gumul-idwé   k-anú   ká   nyúmbá yá
       12-demolish-nom 12SM-your   12SM-assoc   9-house 9SM-assoc
       mkángo k-a-tí-khúmudwíts-a.
       3-lion 12SM-perf-1ˢᵗ pl-disappoint-fv
       'Your manner of demolishing the lion's house has disappointed us.'

(8)   Ma-lim-idwe   anú   á   mundá wá   mkángo
       6-cultivate-nom 6SM-your 6-assoc   3-garden 3SM-assoc 3-lion
       a-a-tí-khúmudwíts-a.
       6SM-perf-1ˢᵗ pl-disappoint-fv
       'Your manner of tilling the lion's garden has disappointed us.'

The suffix ending in these nominalizations is similar to that of the passive in Chichewa. It is arguable that it should indeed be identified with passive morphology since the nominals can take an agentive "*by* phrase." This is illustrated by the following:

(9)   Ka-gumul-idwe   ká   makólá á   mbuzí ndí mkángo
       12-demolish-nom 12SM-assoc   6-corrals 6SM-assoc 10-goats by 3-lion
       sí-ká-ná-sangaláts-é   alenje.
       neg-12SM-pst-please-subjun   2-hunters
       'The manner of demolishing the goats' corrals by the lion did not please the
       hunters.'

In this regard this construction could be compared to such nominals as 'the destruction of the city by the enemy' (cf. Chomsky 1972; Fiengo and Lasnik 1973). The significance of identifying the extension with the passive morpheme is that such nominalizations apply to intransitive verbs too. Admittedly, in such constructions the agentive "*by* phrase" cannot be included. Consider the following:

(10) a. Ma-gon-edw-e á   mwaná uyu á-ma-ti-sowéts-á   mtendele.
         6-sleep-nom   6SM-assoc 1-child this 1SM-hab-1st pl-deprive-fv 3-peace
         'This child's way of sleeping deprives us of peace of mind.'

It should be noted that this nominalization, when applied to intransitive verbs, applies equally to intransitive verbs whose sole argument is patientlike (unaccusatives) and those whose sole argument is agentlike (unergative). Thus, verbs such as *yend-a* 'walk, move,' *sek-a* 'laugh,' *lil-a* 'cry,' and *thamáng-a* 'run' yield such manner nominalizations as *kayendedwe, kasekedwe, kalilidwe*, and *mathamangidwe*. Intransitive verbs whose sole argument is non-agentive (unaccusatives), such as *gw-a* 'fall,' *f-a* 'die,' and *dwal-a* 'be ill,' yield the nominalizations *kagwedwe, kafedwe*, and *kadwalidwe*.

One fact about this nominalization process is that it applies differently to reflexives and reciprocals. The variable treatment is to be expected in light of the domain of its application. Manner nominalization applies to verb stems, and does not include verbal prefixes or clitics. The following examples illustrate the point:

b. Ka-siy-an-idwe   k-áthu   ka-na-ndí-dándául-ĭts-a.
    12-leave-recip-nom 12SM-our 12SM-pst-1st OM-be sad-caus-fv
    'The way we left each other (parted) made me sad.'

In this the nominalization is of a verb that has been reciprocalized. While verbs with the reciprocal can undergo this nominalization process, reflexives, along with OMs in general, do not. This is shown below:

c. *Ka-dzi-met-edwe   ká   mikángo ká-ma-sek-éts-á   afísi.
    12-reflex-shave-nom 12SM-assoc 4-lions   12SM-hab-laugh-caus-fv 2-hyenas
    'The way the lions shave themselves makes the hyenas laugh.'

The process yields comparable results with all other OMs. This may have some relevance to the earlier discussion concerning the reflexive and the reciprocal although no further comment on the matter will be made here.

The observation that passive morphology is available for use in such nominalizations, and that the nominalizing suffix could be attached to intransitive verbs, led to the view that the attachment of passive morphology to verbs should be separated from the application of the transformational rule of Passive. As evidenced by verbs denoting bodily functions such as getting sexually aroused, or involuntary urinating which, although intransitive, could take passive morphology, this nominalization process provides further evidence of the independence of the morphological affixation from syntactic derivation. These observations constituted part of the grounds for Mchombo to formulate and argue for a lexical derivation of passive constructions (Mchombo 1978). The lexical analysis of the passive led to a lexical account of the other syntactic processes whose overt morphological encoding interacts with the passive. In brief, the processes that are morphologically signaled by verb extensions were analyzed as purely lexical. These are the processes that, *inter alia*, affect argument structure. These include the causative, applicative, reciprocal, stative, etc. It was a short step from the conclusion that such processes are lexical, hence do not involve syntactic movement of phrasal constituents, to the articulation of a lexical theory of grammar. These analyses have contributed to the work on the theory of lexical functional grammar (Bresnan 2001; Dalrymple 2001; Falk 2001).

7.4   Compounding

The derivation of nominals in Chichewa is also achieved through compounding. The commonest form of compounding is that which takes a verb and its unmodified object noun or locative noun and creates a noun by adding an appropriate prefix. This is illustrated by the following:

(11)   ph-a dzúwa 'kill the sun'   chi-phadzúwa 'beautiful woman'
        sw-a bumbu 'smash vulva'   chi-swábumbu 'vulva-breaker (large penis)'
        tol-a nkhâni 'pick up news'   m-tolankhâni 'reporter'
        pal-a matábwa 'scrape timber'   m-palamatabwa 'carpenter'
        low-a m'málo 'enter in place'   m-lowammalo 'substitute, pronoun'
        gon-á m'báwa 'sleep in bar'   chi-gonambáwa 'a drunk, an alcoholic'

Cases of noun–noun compounding, while not impossible, are less common. There are examples such as *bókó-munthu* 'hippo-person = a human hippo,' *mnyanjá-sanga* 'lakedweller-savanna grass = a lake dweller lacking fishing expertise, like someone from the savanna hinterland,' *mtóngá-chiwále* 'a tonga person-palm fronds = a tonga person who lives in the palm fronds, i.e. not a real Tonga,' *msungi-chúma* 'keeper-wealth = treasurer.' This is a rare case where the compound noun derives from the verb phrase *sung-a chúma* 'keep wealth.' Instead of the compound-noun formation adhering to the pattern indicated above, an actor noun was derived from the verb, yielding *msungi* 'keeper.' Then that got compounded with the noun *chúma* 'wealth.'

The common compound-noun formation, involving a verb and its unmodified object noun or locative, is subject to restriction. Basically, the object noun cannot be complex, containing a head noun that has a complement, or a noun that is head of a relative-clause construction. The following are therefore ungrammatical:

(12)   *Tola nkhání   zi-méné   anyaní   á-má-fálǐts-a.
        pick 10-news 10SM-rel 2-baboons 2SM-hab-spread-fv
        *M-tolankhání ziméné anyaní ámáfálǐtsa.

In fact, observe the contrast provided by the following minimal pair:

(13) a.   mtolankhaní wá   akazitápe
          1-reporter   1SM-assoc 2-spies
          'the spies' reporter'

     b.   *mtolankhaní zá   akazitápe
          1-reporter   10SM-assoc 2-spies
          'reporter of news about spies (news-about-spies reporter)'

In (13a) the associative marker agrees with the class marker of reporter. In the ungrammatical example (13b), the nominalizing prefix for class 1 *m-* is prefixed to the genitive construction *nkhání zá akazitápe* 'news of the spies.' In other words, it is a nominalization of *tola nkhání zá akazitápe* 'pick up the news of/about the spies.' The intended reading of someone who reports on news about spies cannot be conveyed by this compound-noun formation.

It is rare for this strategy of compound formation to be used with verbs with double objects. It is not clear whether the difficulty arises from grammatical constraints on such nominalizations or whether it is reducible to performance factors. Consider expressions such as *phik-its-á anyaní maúngu* 'make the baboons cook pumpkins' involving the causative, or *phik-il-á anyaní maúngu* 'cook pumpkins for the baboons,' with the applicative. The nominals **mphikitsá anyaní maúngu* 'someone who makes the baboons cook pumpkins' and **mphikilá anyaní maúngu* 'someone who cooks pumpkins for the baboons' are ungrammatical. In fact, even with the ditransitive verb *pats-a* 'give' one does not get *mpatsá njovu maúngu* 'pumpkin giver to elephants' from the verb phrase *patsá njovu maungu* 'give elephants (some) pumpkins.'

7.5   Morpheme order in the verb stem

The issue of constant scholarly interest in Bantu linguistics relates to the determination of constraints on morpheme order in the verb stem. Unlike the clitics or inflectional morphemes, whose order is fairly rigid, the verb-stem suffixes allow for variable ordering, within limits. The questions surrounding the ordering of the suffixes involve the following:

(i)   Is the order determined by principles of syntax?

(ii)   Is the order determined by considerations of semantic composition or semantic scope?

(iii) Is the order determined by principles other than those operative in either syntactic derivation or semantic scope?

The most influential proposal about morpheme ordering in agglutinative languages was the Mirror Principle formulated by Mark Baker (Baker 1985, 1988a). Adopting a classical version of the theory of transformational grammar, Baker observed the nature of fit between syntactic derivation and morpheme order. The emergent pattern appeared to be consistently one of a close fit between the two. In other words, assuming that the application of a transformational rule was overtly marked not just by the rearrangement of the constituents of the sentence but, further, by morphological marking on the verb, the order of the morphemes seemed to correlate with the derivational history of the structure. Morphological ordering seemed to "mirror" syntactic derivation. This led him to formulate the Mirror Principle which states that "morphological derivations must directly reflect syntactic derivations (and vice versa)" (Baker 1985: 375). The Mirror Principle effectively "limits the class of possible morphological structures and how they may be related to syntactic structures in a way that seems to be correct universally" (1985: 375).

To the extent that the Mirror Principle captured relations between morphology and syntax in natural language, it had far-reaching consequences. Baker argued that if syntax and morphology are distinct aspects of linguistic representation, then it should be more than curious that the principles operative in the domain of morphology must pay such close attention to, or be so heavily influenced by, those operative in the domain of syntax. The inescapable conclusion was they were different facets of the same process. The process in question was syntactic, hence morphology was an aspect of syntax. Verb-stem morphotactics in Bantu should, therefore, be sensitive to syntactic constraints.

Baker's conclusion is not inevitable and it has, understandably, drawn a lot of attention especially from critics (cf. Alsina 1990). These point to cases where the syntactic derivation predicts one order but the morphemes appear in a different order. A relevant example here is the order of the applicative and the reciprocal in Chichewa. In the previous chapter it was noted that there appears to be an ordering restriction between these two affixes such that the applicative precedes the reciprocal. The Mirror Principle predicts this but only in the case of the benefactive applicative. Consider the following:

(14)   Anyaní   a-ku-gúl-íl-án-á   mikánda.
        2-baboons 2SM-pres-buy-appl-recip-fv 4-beads
        'The baboons are buying each other some beads.'

In this example, the applicative, encoding 'buy for,' is attached first. The reciprocal, which adds who the beads are bought for, is added later. The order of the two affixes is as expected or predicted by the derivational history of the construction. Now, recall that the applicative can also encode location. In an event where the baboons are pushing each other into a pool, the prediction would be that the verb conveying 'push each other' would be formed first. Then one can add the location where that is occurring. The sentence should be as in (15a):

(15) a.   ?*Anyaní   a-ku-kánkh-án-íl-á   m(u)   dziwe
           2-baboons   2SM-pres-push-recip-appl-fv   16-loc 5-pool

This construction is, at best, questionable. The problem is that the applicative is constrained not to appear directly after the reciprocal. The grammatical version given in (15b) is one in which the order of the two affixes is like that in (14) above:

       b.   Anyaní   a-ku-kánkh-íl-án-á   m(u)   dziwe.
             2-baboons 2SM-pres-push-appl-recip-fv   16-loc 5-pool
             'The baboons are pushing each other into the pool.'

For some speakers, if the order must remain faithful to semantic compositionality, then the reciprocal is redundantly repeated after the applicative. This is illustrated in (15c):

       c.   Anyaní   a-ku-kánkh-án-íl-an-á   m(u)   dziwe.
             2-baboons 2SM-pres-push-recip-appl-recip-fv   16-loc 5-pool
             'The baboons are pushing each other into the pool.'

The situation remains the same even when the applicative introduces an instrument. Consider the following examples:

       d.   Anyaní   a-ku-báy-án-a   ndí   mipálilo.
             2-baboons 2SM-pres-stab-recip-fv   with   4-arrows
             'The baboons are stabbing each other with arrows.'

       e.   Anyaní   a-ku-báy-íl-an-a   mipálilo.
             2-baboons 2SM-pres-stab-appl-recip-fv   4-arrows
             'The baboons are stabbing each other with arrows.'
             Also: 'The baboons are stabbing arrows for each other.'

Other cases where the Mirror Principle appears to hold rather tenuously is in the ordering of the causative and the applicative. In Chichewa the order remains strictly that of causative before applicative.

(16) a.   Anyaní   a-ku-gúl-íts-il-a   mikángó   mikánda.
           2-baboons 2SM-pres-buy-caus-appl-fv   4-lions   4-beads
           'The baboons are selling beads for the lions.'

       b.   ?*Anyaní   a-ku-gúl-íl-íts-á   mikángó   mikánda
             2-baboons 2SM-pres-buy-appl-caus-fv   4-lions   4-beads

Sentence (16b) is ungrammatical or, at best, marginal. However, there is nothing incoherent about its semantic interpretation. The order of the morphemes should be able to yield the reading that the baboons are causing someone to buy beads for the lions. Yet despite the prediction, which is consistent with the Mirror Principle, the structure is not possible. In this respect, the causative–applicative interaction differs from that of the causative and reciprocal. These two can appear in either order, depending on semantic composition. Take the following:

(17) a.   Anyani   a-ku-mény-àn-its-a   mikàngo.
          2-baboons 2SM-pres-hit-recip-caus-fv 4-lions
          'The baboons are making the lions hit each other (fight).'

     b.   Anyaní   a-ku-mény-éts-án-a   mikángo.
          2-baboons 2SM-pres-hit-caus-recip-fv 4-lions
          'The baboons are making the lions make each other hit something.'

Significantly, sentence (17b) appears to be ambiguous between the two interpretations of causing each other to hit and causing to hit each other. This attests to a preference in the morpheme ordering, namely, that the preferred order is that of causative before reciprocal. Still, unlike the case of the applicative, the causative–reciprocal interaction could be viewed as consistent with the Mirror Principle. The ordering restrictions noted certainly undermine the general import of the Mirror Principle. In fact, similar conclusions have been reached about the Mirror Principle on the basis of Xhosa. In a detailed study of argument-structure-reducing processes in Xhosa, with some attention focused on morpheme co-occurrence restrictions, Dlayedwa (2002) has noted that in Xhosa, reciprocalized monotransitive as well as reciprocalized ditransitive verbs are compatible with the passive suffix. The passive suffix in Xhosa is realized by -w- while the reciprocal is realized by the suffix -an-, just as in Chichewa. They co-occur in what she has termed impersonal constructions. These are constructions that lack a (thematic) subject. Now, although the construction is predicted to be reciprocal before passive, it is actually morphologically attested with the opposite morpheme order (i.e. -w-an-). This is illustrated by the following examples:

(18) a.   Ku-ya-leq-w-an-a   ng-ukhetsha nentshontsho.
          imp-SM-pres-VR-pass-recip-fv by hawk   and chicken
          'The hawk and chicken chased each other.'
          (Lit.'It is chased each other by hawk and chicken).'

     b.   Ku-nik-w-an-a   intshontsho ng-ukhetsha no-nomyayi.
          imp-SM-VR-pass-recip-fv 5: chicken   by hawk   and black crow
          'The hawk and the crow gave each other a chicken.'
          (Lit.'It is given each other a chicken by the hawk and the crow.')

She then goes on to point out that "[S]imilar to the reciprocalized productive and mono-transitive verbs, the reciprocalized causative intransitive verb *ba-w-is-en-e* 'have caused each other to fall' together with the reciprocalized applicative verb *ba-w-el-en-e* 'have fallen for each other' also feed passive," as shown in (19a and b):

(19) a.   Ku-w-is-w-en-e   ng-ukhetsha nentshontsho.
           imp-SM-VR-caus-pass-recip-fv   by hawk   and chicken
           'The hawk and the chicken caused each other to fall.'
           (Lit. 'It is caused each other to fall by the hawk and the chicken.')

     b.   Kw-a-w-el-w-an-a   ng-ukhetsha nentshontsho.
           imp-SM-past-VR-appl-pass-recip-fv by hawk   and chicken
           'The hawk and the chicken have fallen for each other.'
           (Lit. 'It was fallen for each other by the hawk and the chicken.')

As stated above, when the passive morpheme is attached to a reciprocalized verb, it precedes the reciprocal suffix. This seems to go against the expected morpheme sequence, which should be the reciprocal before the passive. Such a morpheme sequence is also predicted by the stipulations of the Mirror Principle, as stated by Baker (1985, 1988a). Baker, in explaining regularities between morphological order and syntactic derivation, noted that morpheme sequences associated with grammatical processes tend to appear in an order that reflects the order of syntactic derivation. The suffix order in the impersonal constructions involving the reciprocal clearly goes against this principle. This raises the question of the extent to which the Mirror Principle holds in accounting for morphological ordering. Syntactic derivation predicts that the order should be reciprocal–passive. Yet, the actual morphological order is passive–reciprocal. The question is, should syntactic derivation be taken to proceed as reflected in the morphological ordering? This would be consistent with the Mirror Principle. However, on the basis of her analysis of the Xhosa morphosyntactic organization, Dlayedwa claims that "this is not the case in Xhosa" (Dlayedwa 2002: 70). In other words, Dlayedwa's analysis of Xhosa morphosyntax indicates that the principles that regulate morphological organization are different from, and independent of, the order of syntactic derivation, contra the Mirror Principle.

7.6   Templatic morphology

The apparent independence of morpheme order from syntactic derivation has led researchers to seek alternative accounts. One such account has been that of positing some kind of morphological template. In the process this also attests to the possible separation of morphological derivation from syntactic derivation. The idea behind templatic morphology reduces to the view that the ordering on morpheme sequences may be determined by morphological principles, independent of either syntactic derivation or semantic composition. In studies of various African languages Hyman (Hyman 1991, 2003) has noted that there is a general order of the affixes in the verb stem, such that the causative normally precedes the applicative. This, in turn, precedes the reciprocal, and this precedes the passive. Denoting this as CARP, for Causative, Applicative, Reciprocal, Passive, the claim is that in the absence of over-riding factors, this is the generally preferred order of the morphemes. Chichewa provides some evidence for this morphological template. Note that the causative always precedes the applicative and, even with the reciprocal, there is always the possibility of the causative–reciprocal receiving an ambiguous interpretation instead of having the reciprocal occur before the causative. The applicative does not precede the causative and the causative–applicative order is exploited to convey the reading that the applicative–causative should encode. The position of the passive, as the final suffix, together with its effects, has occasionally raised doubt regarding its status as being a morpholexical as opposed to a morphosyntactic process (see Sadler and Spencer 1998; for response, see Mchombo 1999a).

Templatic morphology avoids the pitfalls of pegging morphological order to syntactic derivation, but it, too, fails to capture all the relevant observations. Consider, for instance, the facts about Xhosa discussed by Dlayedwa and provided above. The impersonal construction in Xhosa may tolerate the passivization of a reciprocalized verb, and this would be consistent with CARP. However, note that the order is that of Passive before Reciprocal, contra CARP. In spite of that, on the whole there is a general preference for morpheme ordering that adheres to the template.

Both templatic morphology and the Mirror Principle could be viewed as offering optimal accounts of morpheme sequences in the verb stem. In other words, in the absence of over-riding factors, the morpheme order will either reflect syntactic derivation or conform to CARP. Morpheme orders that are deviant, in the sense that they do not conform to the general pattern, could be handled either in a manner comparable to accounts of bracketing paradox (cf. Kiparsky 1982a, b; Marantz 1989; Pesetsky 1985; Sproat 1988), or as involving a reranking of constraints in an Optimality Theoretic-analysis. An analysis that appeals to bracketing paradox would be undesirable for the adherents of the Mirror Principle. Pesetsky (1985) proposed a separation of morphological form from semantic structure. Principles of semantic composition hold at the level of logical form. Semantic organization is encoded in overt form by morphological elements. Principles of morphological structure are separate and they apply to morphological structure. The two sets of principles need not operate on structural representations that are isomorphic.

Naturally, to the extent that morphology and logical form are isomorphic, it would make for facilitation of computation of the semantics from morphological form. But there is no requirement in principle that the two coincide, hence bracketing paradoxes arise where the bracketing required for semantic scope differs from the bracketing of constituents on morphological grounds. Note, further, that clitics also introduce lack of isomorphism between syntactic structure and order in phonological representation.

In a sense, the Mirror Principle could be susceptible to similar reformulation. The morpheme sequences that stand in violation of syntactic derivation could be taken to reflect the difference between syntactic and morphological requirements. This would be tantamount to reinstating morphology as separate from syntax, each with its own principles and ordering requirements, a conclusion that Baker rejected. He opted for the elimination of morphology as a separate level of linguistic representation, arguing that morphological derivation is an aspect of syntactic derivation. The problems that variable morpheme ordering raises for the Mirror Principle equally apply to templatic morphology. The difference is that the latter does not try to assimilate morphology to syntax. Still, when the expected order is violated, one is forced to revisit the question of constraints on morpheme sequencing in the verb stem. Note that in some languages, e.g. Xhosa, unlike in Chichewa, the applicative can be suffixed to a reciprocal verb, again contra CARP (cf. Dlayedwa 2002; Satyo 1985). Dlayedwa illustrates this with the following example:

(20)   Ukhetsha ne-ntshontsho ba-leq-en-el-e   abantwana.
        Hawk   and-chicken   2: SM-VR-recip-appl-fv 2: children
        'The hawk and the chicken chase each other for the children.'

In Xhosa "the reciprocal feeds all four suffixes namely the neuter, passive, causative and applicative" (Dlayedwa 2002: 78). An accumulation of cases that depart from the putative norms demands some other way of dealing with the facts.

7.7   Thematic conditions on verbal suffixation in Chichewa

A recurrent pattern in the ordering of the morphemes is that the causative affix tends to precede all other suffixes, and the applicative tends to be the next one. The reciprocal, the stative (or neuter, to use Dlayedwa's terminology), and the passive, all tend to be suffixed after those two. This pattern, captured in templatic morphology, is significant in its correlation with the functions of the affixes. The causative and the applicative are argument-structure-increasing affixes, creating monotransitive or double-object constructions. The remaining affixes are argument-structure-reducing morphemes. Of the argument-structure-increasing morphemes, the causative introduces a new agent, an external argument, and the applicative introduces internal arguments. There is some correspondence in the order of the morphemes to the placement of the roles associated with the introduced arguments on the thematic hierarchy. This leads to speculation that perhaps the thematic hierarchy might play a role in the determination of morpheme order.

This ordering constraint is general in Xhosa in that the affixes of the causative and the applicative, which are valency-increasing processes, normally precede the affixes realizing argument-reducing processes, such as the reciprocal, the passive, etc.

Such constraints on morphological ordering, which do not match semantic reading, have been noted for other languages too (cf. Hyman and Katamba 1990). It is tempting to try and derive this from general principles. It is not clear whether the difference in the prominence of thematic roles associated with these processes has some bearing on the morpheme-ordering restrictions. What it shows is that morpheme ordering may be regulated by principles that are independent of syntactic derivation or semantic scope. The possibility of invoking thematic role information and the thematic hierarchy to account for morpheme ordering sounds appealing but it, too, remains inconclusive. For instance, in our discussion of the stative in Chichewa it was noted that the stative requires appeal to configurations that have such thematic roles as agent and patient/theme. Clearly, this suggests that these notions have a theoretical status within grammatical theory. Thematic roles are abstractions over, or are aspects of, verb semantics that are accessible to syntactic operations. In the interaction of the stative and the applicative there was suggestion that thematic organization seems to regulate morphological co-occurrence. Thus, the stative does not get suffixed to the applicative irrespective of the thematic role that the applicative encodes. The cases of such ordering, not common, but possible among some speakers of some dialects, involve the suffixation of the stative to the benefactive applicative. Thus, for these speakers, expressions such as the following are marginally possible.

(21) a. ?Aná   ó-gúl-íl-ík-á   chipónde
         2-children 2SM-assoc-buy-appl-stat-fv 7-peanut butter
         'Children who can be bought peanut butter'

    b. ?Anyaní   ó-b-él-ék-á   mikánda
         2-baboons 2SM-assoc-steal-appl-stat-fv 4-beads
         'Baboons that could be stolen beads for'

There is one complication in these cases which is that the expressions seem to be like relative clauses. The situation is definitely worse when one tries a simple declarative sentence with the applicative–stative order. Contrast the sentences in (21a and b) with the following:

	c.	*Anyaní	a-ku-gúl-íl-ík-á		mikánda
		2-baboons	2SM-pres-buy-appl-stat-fv		4-beads
	d.	*Anyaní	a-ku-b-él-ék-á		mikánda
		2-baboons	2SM-pres-steal-appl-stat-fv		4-beads

As indicated, this is not common among most speakers of Chichewa and other verbs do not tolerate it as much. In so far as it is possible, it remains significant in ways that will be reviewed below. However, the applicative can be attached to the stative but with some restrictions over the thematic roles that can be associated with such applicatives. The beneficiary applicative or instrumental applicative cannot be formed out of a stative verb, as already noted. Only the applicatives associated with the locative, circumstantial, or malefactive readings are allowed in these cases. This is exemplified by the following:

(22) a.	Mautá awá	a-na-pínd-ík-il-á	pa	chulu.
	6-bows 6-these	6SM-pst-bend-stat-appl-fv	17-on	7-anthill
		'These bows got bent (while) on the anthill.'		
b.	Mautá awá	a-a-pind-ik-il-á	phúzo.	
	6-bows 6-these	6SM-perf-bend-stat-appl-fv	5-spite	
		'These bows got bent out of spite.'		

In these two examples the applicative encodes the locative and the reason/circumstantial respectively. The other usage of the applicative in some Bantu languages is to convey a malefactive reading. Ordinarily, the malefactive argument is expressed by the object marker (OM), with the full NP expressed as a topic to which the OM is anaphorically bound. The malefactive reading of the stative–applicative is shown in the following:

(23)	Mautá ánú	a-a-tí-pínd-ik-ĭl-a.
	6-bows 6-your	6SM-perf-us-bend-stat-appl-fv
		'Your bows have got bent on us.'

The obvious question that arises in connection with these examples is, are there any principles that account for these facts? Are these principles language-particular or do they have cross-linguistic validity? It seems that the principles that regulate these distributional facts apply cross-linguistically. It has been noted in Hausa, a Chadic language, that the applicatives that are obtained from unaccusatives mark the malefactive. This parallels certain aspects of Bantu linguistic structure. The following examples, taken from Bature (1991), illustrate the point:

(24) a.	Motar ta	lalace	wa	Audud.
	car-the it-pst	damage	for/on	Audu
	'The car broke on Audu.'			

b. Agogon ya   tsaya wa   yaron.
    watch   it-pst stop for/on boy-the
    'The watch stopped on the boy.'

c. Karen ya   macee wa maharbin.
    dog   he-pst die   for hunter-the
    'The dog died on the hunter.'

Bature claims that in Hausa the *wa* is phonologically and syntactically bound to the verb. It is not a clitic or a preposition. He adduces a lot of evidence from phonological, morphological, syntactic considerations to show that *wa* is simply an applicative morpheme, in all relevant respects comparable to the applicative morpheme in Bantu languages (see Munkaila 1990).

These facts call for the articulation of general principles that could be plausible candidates for inclusion in the principles of Universal Grammar. One serious attempt at dealing with such facts in linguistic theory would be that of adopting Baker's Mirror Principle but, as pointed out above, the Mirror Principle appears to run into difficulties with some facts about applicatives in Chichewa (cf. Alsina and Mchombo 1990, 1991). Appeal to semantic composition or scope relations equally runs into problems in those cases where the scope relations predict one order of the morphemes but the actual grammatical sequence turns out to be different (cf. Hyman and Mchombo 1992; Rugemalira 1993b). An alternative account that appears to be a perfectly viable proposal for the explanation of these facts, to be reviewed here, is the one that appeals to thematic role structure.

Theories that recognize thematic roles have also shared the view that these roles are hierarchically ordered or, as suggested in some versions of Construction Grammar, that in the argument structure of a predicate there is one argument that is "distinguished." The distinguished argument behaves like a variable over thematic frames. In a frame with an agent and a patient, the distinguished argument will pick out or get paired with the agent (Paul Kay p.c). The thematic frames are schematizations of framal participants. These are then mapped onto thematic roles, which, in turn, get mapped onto grammatical functions. This view is practically translatable into the tripartite division of levels of representation into the lexical conceptual structure, thematic structure, and functional structure, proposed by Jackendoff (1987), with general procedures for mapping the lexical conceptual structure onto the thematic structure and the latter onto the functional structure. Bature (1991) adopts the Jackendovian approach and proposes to handle middle constructions in Hausa, and statives as well, in which the agent role is entirely eliminated and is syntactically inactive, by positing rules that can apply at the stage of mapping the lexical conceptual structure onto thematic structure. Any argument eliminated at this level will not have any syntactic realization, not even as an implicit argument. On the other hand, rules that affect the mapping of thematic structure onto the functional structure may suppress a role although it remains syntactically active, as evidenced by control constructions, and may be realized as obliques (cf. Dubinsky and Simango 1996).

The two important issues that arise from this account are:

(i)   the appeal to thematic roles to account for certain aspects of morphological structure;

(ii)   the idea that thematic roles are hierarchically ordered.

This latter is clearly implicit in the Construction Grammar account (cf. Goldberg 1992). The distinguished argument in effect associates with the most prominent thematic role in the thematic frame. In the discussion of the stative above it was observed that while the idea of a thematic hierarchy has been adopted in a number of theories, the specific details of what the hierarchy looks like have been the locus of controversy. For instance, Alsina and Mchombo (1990), Bresnan and Kanerva (1989), and Bresnan and Moshi (1990) have proposed a hierarchy that looks roughly as follows:

agent > ben > goal/experiencer > instrument > patient/theme > locative

where the symbol ">" is to be read as "is higher than" or "is more prominent than." This conception of the thematic hierarchy is criticized by Baker who, on the basis of data from Sesotho, another Bantu language, claims that there is

> evidence that the benefactive and location constitute a natural class within the theory of semantic roles. The two are indeed a natural class in the Jackendovian approach . . . In contrast, benefactive and locative do not form a natural class in the thematic hierarchy adopted in Alsina and Mchombo and related work. On the contrary, benefactive is one of the "higher" thematic roles, whereas location is the lowest. I consider this to be an advantage of the Jackendovian system of thematic roles.   (Baker 1991: 11)

The view concerning the thematic hierarchy that Baker is critical of, which led him to favor Jackendoff's system of thematic roles, was reviewed and countered in other work. Bresnan and Kanerva critically evaluated the evidence from Jackendoff, and concluded that "neither of Jackendoff's arguments hold up for ordering locative ahead of theme in the thematic hierarchy" (Bresnan and Kanerva 1992: 116).

Regardless of the specifics, it seems to be the case that the facts surrounding the interaction of the stative and the applicative in Chichewa could be claimed to be sensitive to thematic information and the thematic hierarchy. For example, it has been argued that in Chichewa when the applicative introduces a benefactive into the thematic structure, the benefactive cannot be the highest role. If it is assumed that the benefactive is higher than the patient/theme, then a number of restrictions on the ordering of the benefactive applicative and the passive or stative immediately receive explanation. If the passive applies before the benefactive applicative, it will suppress the agent, making the patient the highest expressed role. Applicativizing that configuration would have the effect of introducing the benefactive as the highest expressed role, violating conditions on its thematic configuration. Since the stative is restricted to applying to configurations with agent and patient/theme in the thematic structure, such that it eliminates the agent, making the patient/theme the sole and highest expressed role, its incompatibility with benefactive applicative simply follows from the stated principles. Comparable restrictions seem to apply to interactions between the stative and instrumental applicatives. On the other hand, if the locative, circumstantial, and maleficiary, are lower than the patient/theme on the thematic hierarchy, then this general principle is simply not invoked, and the co-occurrence is permitted. The viability of this proposal strongly suggests the need for a thematic hierarchy, and suggests that the benefactive and the locative should indeed be kept separate, with the locative lower on the hierarchy than the patient/theme, contra Baker. It also argues for the separation of the malefactive from the benefactive, the two appearing on different sides of the patient/theme role in the hierarchy. This also resolves a query concerning the separability of the benefactive from the malefactive raised by Harford (1989) for Chishona. While the determination of the exact place that the malefactive occupies on the thematic hierarchy has to be satisfactorily resolved, the question of its independence from the benefactive cannot remain in doubt. A revised version of the thematic hierarchy, as hinted at in the works of Bature (1991) and Hyman and Mchombo (1992), might look as follows:

agent>ben>goal/exp>instrument>patient/theme>locative>malefactive>circumstantial

The conclusion arrived at here is that aspects of constraints on morpheme ordering in the verb stem in Chichewa appeal to thematic information and the thematic hierarchy. If this is indeed the case, then it clearly suggests one fruitful line of inquiry into semantic constraints on syntactic processes and the nature of the contribution of semantics to syntactic organization. In turn, this argues for the recognition of thematic roles as necessary entities within linguistic theory. Naturally, the question of the generality with which thematic information may constrain syntactic structure or syntactic processes is a topic that merits serious investigation (cf. Alsina and Mchombo 1991; Baker 1991; Bature 1991; Hyman and Mchombo 1992, to name only a few). The success of this program would obviously indicate that the skepticism towards the presence of, and need for, thematic roles in linguistic theory (cf. Ravin 1990) is misguided. It seems to be the case that the stative construction in Chichewa and other languages proves to be a very useful probe into the issues pertaining to the relevance of thematic information in linguistic theory, and to the nature of constraints on morpheme ordering in the verb stem.

In the final analysis, regardless of which approach is deemed most suitable for accounting for morpheme order in the verb stem in Bantu, it is clear that the verb stem remains the domain of significant linguistic processes. The processes do not extend to the elements that are outside it, the clitics. These have been shown to be formally and functionally different from the affixes that affect argument structure and are within the verb stem.

7.8   Conclusion

This chapter has focused on the verb stem, highlighting its status as the domain of significant linguistic processes. The morphological organization of the verb in Bantu provides for a substructure, the verb stem. It has lexical integrity and is, arguably, a unit of lexical processes, not the least of which are processes affecting predicate–argument structure. It is the locus of phonological, morphological, syntactic, and semantic processes, all of which attest to its lexical integrity. As a matter of fact, the issue of lexical integrity and pronominal incorporation received detailed discussion in Bresnan and Mchombo (1995). There, derivational and inflectional affixation are distinguished in explaining anaphoric island effects. The verb unit also includes elements that are attached to the verb stem. These have a different status, being more oriented toward clause structure. The architecture of grammatical theory should provide for the capturing of these facets and providing an explanation of them that fits them into studies of human cognition.

References

Abasheikh, Mohammad I. (1978) "The Grammar of Chimwini Causatives." Doctoral dissertation, University of Illinois at Urbana-Champaign.

Aboh, Enoch Oladé (1999) "From the Syntax of Gungbe to the Grammar of Gbe." Doctoral dissertation, Université de Genève.

Allan, Keith (1983) "Anaphora, Cataphora, and Topic Focusing: Functions of the Object Prefix in Swahili." In *Current Approaches to African Linguistics* 1, ed. Ivan R. Dihoff, 323–335. Dordrecht: Foris Publications.

Alsina, Alex (1990) "Where's the Mirror Principle? Evidence from Chichewa." Paper presented at the 13th Generative Linguistics in the Old World (GLOW) Colloquium at St. John's College, Cambridge University, April 6–8.

(1992) "On the Argument Structure of Causatives." *Linguistic Inquiry* 23: 517–555.

(1993) "Predicate Composition: A Theory of Syntactic Function Alternations." Doctoral dissertation, Stanford University.

(1994) "Bantu Multiple Objects: Analyses and Fallacies." *Linguistic Analysis* 24: 153–174.

(1996a) "Passive Types and the Theory of Object Asymmetries." *Natural Language and Linguistic Theory* 14: 673–723.

(1996b) *The Role of Argument Structure in Grammar*. Stanford, CA: Center for the Study of Language and Information.

(1997) "Causatives in Bantu and Romance." In *Complex Predicates*, ed. Alex Alsina, Joan Bresnan, and Peter Sells, 203–246. Stanford, CA: CSLI Publications.

Alsina, Alex, Joan Bresnan, and Peter Sells (eds.) (1997) *Complex Predicates*. Stanford, CA: CSLI Publications.

Alsina, Alex, and Smita Joshi (1991) "Parameters in Causative Constructions." *Proceedings of the Chicago Linguistic Society* 27: 1–15.

Alsina, Alex, and Sam A. Mchombo (1990) "The Syntax of Applicatives in Chichewa: Problems for a Theta-theoretic Asymmetry." *Natural Language and Linguistic Theory* 8: 493–506.

(1991) "Object Extraction and the Accessibility of Thematic Information." Paper delivered at the Berkeley Linguistics Society, Berkeley, CA.

(1993) "Object Asymmetries and the Chichewa Applicative Construction." In *Theoretical Aspects of Bantu Grammar*, ed. Sam A. Mchombo, 17–45. Stanford, CA: CSLI Publications.

Anderson, Stephen R. (1985) "Inflectional Morphology." In *Language Typology and Syntactic Description III. Grammatical Categories and the Lexicon*, ed. Timothy Shopen, 150–201. London: Cambridge University Press.

(1988) "Inflection." In *Theoretical Morphology: Approaches in Modern Linguistics*, ed. Michael Hammond and Michael Noonan, 23–44. San Diego, CA: Academic Press.

Ashton, Ethel O. (1947) *Swahili Grammar (Including Intonation)*. London: Longmans, Green and Co.

Austin, Peter, and Joan Bresnan (1996) "Non-Configurationality in Australian Aboriginal Languages." *Natural Language and Linguistic Theory* 14, no. 2: 215–268.

Bach, Emmon, Joan Bresnan, and Thomas Wasow (1974) "Sloppy Identity: An Unnecessary and Insufficient Criterion for Deletion Rules." *Linguistic Inquiry* 5: 609–614.

Baker, Mark (1985) "The Mirror Principle and Morphosyntactic Explanation." *Linguistic Inquiry* 16, no. 3: 373–415.

(1988a) *Incorporation: A Theory of Grammatical Function Changing*. Chicago: University of Chicago Press.

(1988b) "Theta Theory and the Syntax of Applicatives in Chichewa." *Natural Language and Linguistic Theory* 6: 353–389.

(1990) "Pronominal Inflection and the Morphology-Syntax Interface." Paper delivered at the 26th Annual Meeting of the Chicago Linguistic Society, Chicago.

(1991) "Some Subject/Object Non-asymmetries in Mohawk." *Natural Language and Linguistic Theory* 9: 537–576.

(1992) "Thematic Conditions on Syntactic Structures: Evidence from Locative Applicatives." In *Thematic Structure: Its Role in Grammar*, ed. Iggy M. Roca, 23–46. Berlin and New York: Foris.

(2003) "Agreement, Dislocation, and Partial Configurationality." In *Formal Approaches to Function in Grammar: in Honour of Eloise Jelinek*, ed. Andrew Carnie, Heidi Harley, and Mary Ann Willie, 107–134. Amsterdam: John Benjamins.

Bature, Abdullahi (1991) "Thematic Arguments and Semantic Roles in Hausa." Doctoral dissertation, Stanford University.

Bentley, Mayrene Elizabeth (1994) "The Syntactic Effects of Animacy in Bantu Languages." Doctoral dissertation, Indiana University.

Bergvall, Victoria (1985) "A Typology of Empty Categories for Kikuyu and Swahili." In *Current Approaches to African Linguistics*, ed. Gerrit Dimmendaal, 3. Dordrecht: Foris.

(1987) "Focus in Kikuyu and Universal Grammar." Doctoral dissertation, Harvard University.

Biloa, Edmond (1990) "Resumptive Pronouns in Tuki." *Studies in African Linguistics* 21: 211–236.

Bleek, Wilhelm H. I. (1862/69) *A Comparative Grammar of South African Languages*. London: Trübner.

Bodomo, Adams B. (1997) "Paths and Pathfinders: Exploring the Syntax and Semantics of Complex Verbal Predicates in Dagaare and Other Languages." Doctoral dissertation, Norwegian University of Science and Technology.

Bokamba, Eyamba (1976) "Question Formation in Some Bantu Languages." Doctoral dissertation, Indiana University.

(1981) "Aspects of Bantu Syntax." Unpublished manuscript, University of Illinois at Urbana-Champaign.

Brame, Michael K. (1976) *Conjectures and Refutations in Syntax and Semantics*. New York: Elsevier North-Holland.

(1983) "Bound Anaphora is not a Relation between NPs." *Linguistic Analysis* 11: 139–166.

(1984) "Universal Word Induction vs. Move α." *Linguistic Analysis* 14: 313–352.

Bresnan, Joan (1978) "A Realistic Transformational Grammar." In *Linguistic Theory and Psychological Reality*, ed. Morris Halle, Joan Bresnan, and George Miller, 1–59. Cambridge, MA: MIT Press.

(1982a) "Control and Complementation." *Linguistic Inquiry* 13: 343–434.

ed. (1982b) *The Mental Representation of Grammatical Relations*. Cambridge, MA: MIT Press.

(1991) "Locative Case vs. Locative Gender." Paper delivered at the Berkeley Linguistics Society, Berkeley, CA.

(1994) "Locative Inversion and the Architecture of Universal Grammar." *Language* 70, no. 1: 72–131.

(1995) "Category Mismatches." In *Theoretical Approaches to African Linguistics*, ed. Akinbiyi Akinlabi, 19–46. Lawrenceville, NJ: Africa World Press.

(2001) *Lexical-Functional Syntax*. Oxford: Blackwell Publishers.

Bresnan, Joan, and Jonni Kanerva (1989) "Locative Inversion in Chichewa: A Case Study of Factorization in Grammar." *Linguistic Inquiry* 20, no. 1: 1–50.

(1992) "The Thematic Hierarchy and Locative Inversion in UG. A Reply to Paul Schachter's Comments." *In Syntax and the Lexicon* (Syntax and Semantics 26), eds. Tim Stowell and E. Wehrli, 111–125. New York: Academic Press.

Bresnan, Joan, and Sam A. Mchombo (1986) "Grammatical and Anaphoric Agreement." Paper delivered at the Parasession on Pragmatics and Grammatical Theory, University of Chicago.

(1987) "Topic, Pronoun and Agreement in Chichewa." *Language* 63, no. 4: 741–782.

(1995) "The Lexical Integrity Principle: Evidence from Bantu." *Natural Language and Linguistic Theory* 13: 181–254.

Bresnan, Joan, and Lioba Moshi (1990) "Object Asymmetries in Comparative Bantu Syntax." *Linguistic Inquiry* 21: 147–185.

Bresnan, Joan, and Annie Zaenen (1990) "Deep Unaccusativity in LFG." In *Grammatical Relations: A Cross-Theoretical Perspective*, ed. Katarzyna Dziwirek, Patrick Farrell, and Errapel Meijas-Bikandi, 45–58. Stanford, CA: CSLI Publications.

Carstens, Vicki (1991) "The Morphology and Syntax of Determiner Phrases in Kiswahili." Doctoral dissertation, University of California at Los Angeles.

Chichewa Board (1990) *Chichewa Orthography Rules*. Zomba, Malawi.

Chimbutane, Feliciano (2002) "Grammatical Functions in Changana: Types, Properties and Function Alternations." M.Phil. dissertation, Australian National University.

Chimombo, Moira, and Al Mtenje (1989) "Interaction of Tone, Syntax and Semantics in the Acquisition of Chichewa Negation." *Studies in African Linguistics* 20, no. 2: 1–26.

(1991) "The Acquisition of Syntactic Tone: The Case of Chichewa Negation." *Journal of Humanities* 5: 53–86.

Chomsky, Noam (1957) *Syntactic Structures*. The Hague: Mouton.

(1965) *Aspects of the Theory of Syntax*. Cambridge, MA: MIT Press.

(1972) *Studies on Semantics in Generative Grammar*. The Hague: Mouton.

(1977) "On WH-Movement." In *Formal Syntax*, ed. Peter W. Culicover, Thomas Wasow, and Adrian Akmajian, 71–132. New York: Academic Press, Inc.

(1980) *Rules and Representations*. New York: Columbia University Press.

(1981) *Lectures on Government and Binding*. Dordrecht: Foris.

(1985) *Knowledge of Language: Its Nature, Origin and Use*. New York: Praeger.

(1991) "Some Notes on Economy of Derivation and Representation." In *Principles and Parameters in Comparative Grammar*, ed. Robert Freidin, 417–454. Cambridge, MA: MIT Press.

Chomsky, Noam, and Howard Lasnik (1977) "Filters and Control." *Linguistic Inquiry* 8: 425–504.

(1993) "Principles and Parameters Theory." In *Syntax: An International Handbook of Contemporary Research*, ed. J. Jacobs, A. von Stechow, W. Sternefeld, and T. Vennemann. Berlin: Walter de Gruyter.

Corbett, Greville, and Al D. Mtenje (1987) "Gender Agreement in Chichewa." *Studies in African Linguistics* 18, no. 1: 1–38.

Dalrymple, Mary (2001) *Lexical-Functional Grammar* (Syntax and Semantics 34). New York: Academic Press.

Dalrymple, Mary, Sam A. Mchombo, and Stanley Peters (1994) "Semantic Similarities and Syntactic Contrasts between Chichewa and English Reciprocals." *Linguistic Inquiry* 25, no. 1: 145–163.

Dalrymple, Mary, Makoto Kanazawa, Sam Mchombo, and Stanley Peters (1994) "What Do Reciprocals Mean?" In *Proceedings of the Fourth Semantics and Linguistic Theory Conference: SALT IV*, ed. Mandy Harvey and Lynn Santelmann. Rochester, NY.

Dalrymple, Mary, Makoto Kanazawa, Yookyung Kim, Sam Mchombo, and Stanley Peters (1998) "Reciprocal Expressions and the Concept of Reciprocity." *Linguistics and Philosophy* 21: 159–210.

de Guzman, V. P. (1987) "Indirect Objects in Siswati." *Studies in African Linguistics* 18: 309–325.

Dembetembe, Norris C. (1987) *A Linguistic Study of the Verb in Korekore*. Harare: University of Zimbabwe.

Demuth, Katherine (1990) "Locatives, Impersonals and Expletives in Sesotho." *The Linguistic Review* 7: 233–249.

Demuth, Katherine, and Mark Johnson (1989) "Interaction Between Discourse Functions and Agreement in Setawana." *Journal of African Languages and Linguistics* 11: 21–35.

Dlayedwa, Cynthia Zodwa (2002) "Valency-reducing Processes in Xhosa." Doctoral dissertation, University of Essex.

Du Plessis, J. A., and Marianna Visser (1992) *Xhosa Syntax*. Pretoria: Via Afrika.

Dubinsky, Stanley, and Silvester Ron Simango (1996) "Passive and Stative in Chichewa: Evidence for Modular Distinctions in Grammar." *Language* 72, no. 4: 749–781.

Everett, Daniel L. (1989) "Clitic Doubling, Reflexives, and Word Order Alternations in Yagua." *Language* 65, no. 2: 339–372.

Falk, Yehuda N. (2001) *Lexical-Functional Grammar: An Introduction to Parallel Constraint-Based Syntax*. Stanford, CA: CSLI Publications.

Fiengo, Robert, and Howard Lasnik (1973) "The Logical Structure of Reciprocal Sentences in English." *Foundations of Language* 9: 447–468.

Firmino, Gregório D. (1995) "Revisiting the 'Language Question' in Post-colonial Africa: The Case of Portuguese and Indigenous Languages in Mozambique." Doctoral dissertation, University of California, Berkeley.

Gary, Judith, and Ed Keenan (1977) "On Collapsing Grammatical Relations in Universal Grammar." In *Grammatical Relations* (Syntax and Semantics 8), ed. Peter Cole and Jerold Sadock, 149–188. New York: Academic Press.

Givón, Talmy (1971) "On the Verbal Origin of the Bantu Verb Suffixes." *Studies in African Linguistics* 2, no. 2: 145–163.

Goldberg, Adele (1992) *In Support of a Semantic Account of Resultatives*. Stanford, CA: CSLI Publications.

Goldsmith, John, and Firmard Sabimana (1985) "The Ki-Rundi Verb." University of Chicago.

Grimshaw, Jane (1982) "On Lexical Representation of Romance Reflexive Clitics." In *The Mental Representation of Grammatical Relations*, ed. Joan Bresnan, 87–148. Cambridge, MA: MIT Press.

(1990) *Argument Structure*. Linguistic Inquiry Monographs 18, ed. Samuel Jay Keyser. Cambridge, MA: MIT Press.

Guthrie, Malcolm (1962) "The Status of Radical Extensions in Bantu Languages." *Journal of African Languages* 1: 202–220.

Hale, Kenneth (1983) "Warlpiri and the Grammar of Non-configurational Languages." *Natural Language and Linguistic Theory* 1: 5–74.

Hale, Ken, and Samuel Jay Keyser (1992) "The Syntactic Character of Thematic Structure." In *Thematic Structure: Its Role in Grammar*, ed. Iggy M. Roca, 107–143. Berlin and New York: Foris.

Hall Partee, Barbara (1971) "On the Requirement that Transformations Preserve Meaning." In *Studies in Linguistic Semantics*, ed. Charles J. Fillmore and D. Terence Langendoen, 1–21. New York: Holt, Rinehart and Winston, Inc.

Halpern, Aaron (1995) *On the Placement and Morphology of Clitics*. Dissertations in Linguistics, ed. Joan Bresnan, Sharon Inkelas, William J. Poser, and Peter Sells. Stanford, CA: CSLI Publications.

(1998) "Clitics." In *The Handbook of Morphology*, ed. Andrew Spencer and Arnold Zwicky, 101–122. Oxford: Blackwell.

Harford, Carolyn (1989) "Locative inversion in Chishona." In *Current Approaches to African Linguistics*, ed. John P. Hutchison and Victor Manfredi, 7: 137–144. Dordrecht: Foris.

(1991) "Object Asymmetries in Kitharaka." Paper delivered at the Special Session on African Language Structures, Berkeley, CA.

(1993) "The Applicative in Chishona and Lexical Mapping Theory." In *Theoretical Aspects of Bantu Grammar*, ed. Sam A. Mchombo, 93–111. Stanford, CA: CSLI Publications.

Haverkort, Marco (1993) "Clitics and Parametrization: Case Studies in the Interaction of Head Movement Phenomena." Doctoral dissertation, Katholieke Universiteit Brabant.

Hoffman, Mika (1991) "The Syntax of Argument-Structure-Changing Morphology." Doctoral dissertation, Massachusetts Institute of Technology.

Horrocks, Geoffrey (1987) *Generative Grammar*. London: Longman.

Huang, C-T. J. (1982) "Logical Relations in Chinese and the Theory of Grammar." Doctoral dissertation, Massachusetts Institute of Technology.

Hyman, Larry (1991) "Conceptual Issues in the Comparative Study of the Bantu Verb Stem." In *Topics in African Linguistics*, ed. Salikoko S. Mufwene and Lioba Moshi, 3–34. Amsterdam and Philadelphia: John Benjamins Publishing Co.

(2003) "Suffix Ordering in Bantu: A Morphocentric Approach." *Yearbook of Morphology 2002*, 245–281.

Hyman, Larry, and Francis Katamba (1990) "Spurious High-tone Extension in Luganda." *Southern Africa Journal of African Languages* 10: 142–158.

(1993) "A New Approach to Tone in Luganda." *Language* 69, no. 1: 34–67.

Hyman, Larry, and Sam A. Mchombo (1992) "Morphotactic Constraints in the Chichewa Verb Stem." Paper delivered at the Parasession on the Place of Morphology in a Grammar, Berkeley, CA.

Jackendoff, Ray (1972) *Semantic Interpretation in Generative Grammar*. Cambridge, MA: MIT Press.

(1987) "The Status of Thematic Relations in Linguistic Theory." *Linguistic Inquiry* 18, no. 3: 369–411.

(1990) *Semantic Structures*. Cambridge, MA: MIT Press.

Jaeggli, Osvaldo (1982) *Topics in Romance Syntax*. Dordrecht: Foris.

Jelinek, Eloise (1984) "Empty Categories, Case, and Configurationality." *Natural Language and Linguistic Theory* 2: 39–76.

Kalipeni, E. (1998) "The Chewa of Malawi." In *Worldmark Encyclopedia of Cultures and Daily Life*, vol. 1: Africa, ed. Timothy L. Gall, 98–102. Detroit, MI: Gale Research Inc.

Kanerva, Jonni M. (1990) *Focus and Phrasing in Chichewa Phonology*. Outstanding Dissertations in Linguistics, ed. Jorge Hankamer. New York: Garland.

Kashoki, M. (1978) "Between-Language Communication in Zambia." In *Language in Zambia*, ed. S. and M. Kashoki Ohannessian. London: International African Institute.

Katamba, Francis (1984) "A Nonlinear Analysis of Vowel Harmony in Luganda." *Journal of Linguistics* 20: 257–275.

Kathol, Andreas, and Richard Rhodes (2000) "Constituency and Linearization of Ojibwa Nominals." In *Proceedings of WSCLA* 4 (UBC Working Papers in Linguistics II), ed. Marion Caldecott, Suzanne Gessner, and Eun-Sook Kim, 75–91. Vancouver: Dept. of Linguistics, University of British Columbia.

Katupha, José Matéus (1991) "The Grammar of Emakhuwa Verbal Extensions." Doctoral dissertation, School of Oriental and African Studies, University of London.

Katz, Jerrold J., and Paul M. Postal (1964) *An Integrated Theory of Linguistic Descriptions*. Cambridge, MA: MIT Press.

Kawasha, Boniface (1999a) "Relativization and Grammatical Relations in Lunda." Department of Linguistics, University of Oregon.

(1999b) "Some Aspects of Lunda Grammar." MA dissertation, University of Oregon.

Keach, Camillia N. (1995) "Subject and Object Markers as Agreement and Pronoun Incorporation in Swahili." In *Theoretical Approaches to African Linguistics*, ed. Akinbiyi Akinlabi, 1, 109–116. Trenton, NJ: Africa World Press, Inc.

Keach, Nikki (1980) "The Syntax and Interpretation of the Relative Clause Construction in Swahili." Doctoral dissertation, University of Massachusetts, Amherst, MA.

Kimenyi, Alexandre (1980) *A Relational Grammar of Kinyarwanda*. Los Angeles: University of California Press.

King, Tracy Holloway (1995) *Configuring Topic and Focus*. Dissertations in Linguistics. Stanford, CA: CSLI Publications.

Kinyalolo, Kasangati (1991) "Syntactic Dependencies and the SPEC-head Agreement Hypothesis in Kilega." Doctoral dissertation, University of California at Los Angeles.

Kiparsky, Paul (1982a) "Lexical Morphology and Phonology." In *Linguistics in the Morning Calm*, ed. the Linguistic Society of Korea, 3–92. Seoul: Hanshin Publishing Company.

(1982b) "Word-Formation and the Lexicon." Unpublished paper, Massachusetts Institute of Technology.

Klavans, Judith L. (1983) "The Morphology of Cliticization." Paper delivered at the Chicago Linguistic Society, Chicago.

Koster, Jan, and Robert May (1982) "On the Constituency of Infinitives." *Language* 58: 116–143.

Kula, Nancy Chongo (2002) *The Phonology of Verbal Derivation in Bemba*. Utrecht: LOT.

Laka, Itziar (1994) *On the Syntax of Negation*. Outstanding Dissertations in Linguistics, ed. Jorge Hankamer. New York and London: Garland Publishing, Inc.

Lakoff, George, and Stanley Peters (1966) "Phrasal Conjunction and Symmetric Predicates." In *Modern Studies in English: Readings in Transformational Grammar*, ed. David Reibel and Sanford Schane. Englewood Cliffs, NJ: Prentice-Hall.

Lee, Sophia Yat Mei (2001) "Complement Functions in Cantonese: A Lexical-Functional Grammar Approach." M. Phil. dissertation, University of Hong Kong.

Lehmann, Dorothea (2002) *An Outline of Cinyanja Grammar*. Lusaka, Zambia: Bookworld Publishers.

Levin, Juliette (1983) "Reduplication and Prosodic Structure." Paper delivered at the GLOW Colloquium, York.

Machobane, Malillo (1989) "Some Restrictions on the Sesotho Transitivizing Morphemes." Doctoral dissertation, McGill University.

(1993) "The Ordering Restriction between the Sesotho Applicative and Causative Suffixes." *South African Journal of African Languages* 13: 129–137.

Marantz, Alec (1982) "Re Reduplication." *Linguistic Inquiry* 13: 435–482.

(1984) *On the Nature of Grammatical Relations*. Cambridge, MA: MIT Press.

(1988) "Clitics, Morphological Merger, and the Mapping to Phonological Structure." In *Theoretical Morphology: Approaches in Modern Linguistics*, ed. Michael Hammond and Michael Noonan, 253–270. San Diego: Academic Press.

(1989) "Clitics and Phrase Structure." In *Alternative Conceptions of Phrase Structure*, ed. Mark R. Baltin and Anthony S. Kroch, 99–116. Chicago: University of Chicago Press.

Marten, Lutz (1999) "Agreement with Conjoined Noun Phrases in Swahili." School of Oriental and African Studies, University of London.

Matambirofa, Francis (2002) "Lexical Mapping Theory Account of the Applicative and Causative Extensions in Shona." Doctoral dissertation, University of Zimbabwe.

Mathangwane, Joyce (1994) "Morphology-Syntax Distinction: Evidence from the Copula Allomorphy in Ikalanga." University of California at Berkeley.

Matsinhe, Sozinho (1994) "The Status of Verbal Affixes in Bantu Languages with Special Reference to Tsonga: Problems and Possibilities." *South African Journal of African Languages* 14, no. 4: 163–176.

Matthewson, Lisa, and Charlotte Reinholtz (1996) "The Syntax and Semantics of Determiners: A Comparison of Salish and Cree." Paper delivered at the International Conference on Salish and Neighbouring Languages, Vancouver.

May, Robert (1985) *Logical Form: Its Structure and Derivation.* Cambridge, MA: MIT Press.

Mchombo, Sam (1978) "A Critical Appraisal of the Place of Derivational Morphology within Transformational Grammar, Considered with Primary Reference to Chichewa and Swahili." Doctoral dissertation, University of London.

(1980) "Dative and Passive in Chichewa: An Argument for Surface Grammar." *Linguistic Analysis* 6, no. 2: 97–113.

(1992) "Reciprocalization in Chichewa: A Lexical Account." *Linguistic Analysis* 21, no. 1–2: 3–22.

(1993a) "A Formal Analysis of the Stative Construction in Bantu." *Journal of African Languages and Linguistics* 14: 5–28.

(1993b) "On the Binding of the Reflexive and the Reciprocal in Chichewa." In *Theoretical Aspects of Bantu Grammar*, ed. Sam A. Mchombo, 181–208. Stanford, CA: CSLI Publications.

ed. (1993c) *Theoretical Aspects of Bantu Grammar.* Stanford, CA: CSLI Publications.

(1997) "Contributions of African Languages to Generative Grammar." In *African Linguistics at the Crossroads: Papers from Kwaluseni*, ed. Robert K. Herbert. Cologne: Rudiger Koppe Verlag.

(1998) "Chichewa (Bantu)." In *Handbook of Morphology*, ed. Andrew Spencer and Arnold Zwicky, 500–520. Oxford: Blackwell.

(1999a) "Argument Structure and Verbal Morphology in Chichewa." *Malilime. Malawian Journal of Linguistics* 1: 57–75.

(1999b) "Quantification and Verb Morphology: The Case of Reciprocals in African Languages." *Linguistic Analysis* 29: 182–213.

(2001a) "Chichewa Verbal Organization and the Study of Cognition." *Malilime. Malawian Journal of Linguistics* 2. 28–46.

(2001b) "Effects of Head-marking on Constituent Order in Chichewa." In *Proceedings of the LFG 01 Conference*, ed. Miriam Butt and Tracy Holloway King, 221–237. Stanford, CA: CSLI Publications.

(2002a) "Affixes, Clitics, and Bantu Morphosyntax." In *Language Universals and Variation*, ed. Mengistu Amberber and Peter Collins, 185–210. Westport, CT: Prager.

(2002b) "Argument Structure, Functional Structure, and the Split Morphology Hypothesis." In *Sexto Encuentro Internacional de Lingüística en el Noroeste*, ed. Zarina Estrada Fernández and Rosa María Ortiz Ciscomani, 29–53. Hermosillo, Mexico: Universidad de Sonora.

(2002c) "Head-marking, Agreement, and Partial Configurationality in Chichewa." Paper presented at the 7th Encuentro Internacional de Lingüística en el Noroeste, Universidad de Sonora, Hermosillo, Mexico.

(2003) "On Discontinuous Constituents in Chichewa." In *Typologie de Langues d'Afrique et Universaux de la Grammaire*, ed. Anne Zribi-Hertz and Patrick Sauzet, 141–167. Paris: L'Harmattan.

Mchombo, Sam A., and Francis Moto (1981) "Tone and the Theory of Syntax." *Studies in African Linguistics* Supplement 8: 92–95.

Mchombo, Sam A., and Al D. Mtenje (1983) "Noncyclic Grammar." *Linguistic Analysis* 11, no. 2: 219–236.

Mchombo, Sam A., and Rosemary M. Ngalande (1980) "Reciprocal Verbs in Chichewa: A Case for Lexical Derivation." *Bulletin of the School of Oriental and African Studies* 45: 570–575.

Mchombo, Sam A., and Armindo S. A. Ngunga (1994) "The Syntax and Semantics of the Reciprocal Construction in Ciyao." *Linguistic Analysis* 24, no. 1–2: 3–31.

McNally, Louise (1993) "Comitative Coordination: A Case Study of Group Formation." *Natural Language and Linguistic Theory* 11: 347–379.

Meeussen, A. E. (1971) "Bantu Grammatical Reconstructions." *Africana Linguistica* 3: 79–122.

Mohanan, K. P. (1986) *The Theory of Lexical Phonology*. Dordrecht: Reidel.

Möhlig, Wilheim J. G., Lutz Marten, and Jekura U. Kavari (2002) *A Grammatical Sketch of Herero (Otjiherero)*. Cologne: Rüdiger Köppe Verlag.

Morimoto, Yukiko (2000) "Discourse Configurationality in Bantu Morphosyntax." Doctoral dissertation, Stanford University.

    (2002) "From Synchrony to Diachrony: Topic Salience and Cross-Linguistic Patterns of Agreement." Heinrich-Heine Universität Düsseldorf, Institut für Sprache und Information.

Mtenje, Al (1980) "Aspects of Chichewa Derivational Phonology and Syllable Structure Constraints." MA dissertation, Southern Illinois University, Carbondale.

    (1985) "Arguments for an Autosegmental Analysis of Chichewa Vowel Harmony." *Lingua* 66: 21–52.

    (1986a) "Remarks on Extra-Harmonicality in Bantu Harmonic Systems." *Sheffield Working Papers in Language and Linguistics* 3: 62–76.

    (1986b) "Issues in the Nonlinear Phonology of Chichewa." Doctoral dissertation, University College London.

    (1987) "Tone Shift Principles in the Chichewa Verb." *Lingua* 72: 169–209.

    (1988) "On Tone and Transfer in Chichewa Reduplication." *Linguistics* 26: 125–155.

Mugane, John (1997) *A Paradigmatic Grammar of Gikuyu*. Stanford, CA: CSLI Publications.

Munkaila, Muhammed M. (1990) "Indirect Object Constructions in Hausa." Doctoral dissertation, School of Oriental and African Studies, University of London.

Mutaka, Ngessimo (1995) *The Lexical Tonology of Kinande*. LINCOM Studies in African Linguistics 01, ed. Francis Katamba. Munich: LINCOM Europa.

Mutaka, Ngessimo, and Larry Hyman (1990) "Syllables and Morpheme Integrity in Kinande Reduplication." *Phonology* 7: 73–119.

Myers, Scott (1991) *Tone and the Structure of Words in Shona*. Outstanding Dissertations in Linguistics, ed. Jorge Hankamer. New York: Garland.

Neale, Stephen (1996) "Prolegomena to a 'Variable-driven' Syntax: Reflections on Logical Form and Chomsky's Minimalist Program." Stanford University.

Newmeyer, Frederick (1974) "The Precyclic Nature of Predicate Raising." Bloomington, Indiana: Indiana University Linguistics Club.

    (1975) "The Position of Incorporation Transformations in Grammar." Paper delivered at the Berkeley Linguistics Society, Berkeley, CA.

Ngonyani, Deogratius (1996) "The Morphosyntax of Applicatives." Doctoral dissertation, University of California at Los Angeles.

(1998a) "Properties of Applied Objects in Kiswahili and Kindendenle." *Studies in African Linguistics* 27, no. 1: 67–95.

(1998b) "V-to-I Movement in Kiswahili." In *AAP Swahili Forum V*, ed. Rose Marie Beck, Thomas Geider, and Werner Graebner, 55, 129–144. Cologne: Institut für Afrikanistik, Universität zu Köln.

(1999) "X° Movement in Kiswahili Relative Clause Verbs." *Linguistic Analysis* 29, no. 1–2: 137–159.

Ngunga, Armindo (2000) *Phonology and Morphology of the Ciyao Verb*. Stanford Monographs in African Languages, ed. William R. Leben and Larry M. Hyman. Stanford, CA: CSLI Publications.

Nordlinger, Rachel (1998) *Constructive Case. Evidence from Australian Languages*. Dissertations in Linguistics. Stanford, CA: CSLI Publications.

Omar, Alwiya S. (1990) "Grammatical and Anaphoric Relations in Kiswahili: Functions of the Subject and Object Prefixes." Unpublished manuscript, Indiana University.

Perlmutter, David (1978) "Impersonal Passives and the Unaccusative Hypothesis." Paper delivered at the Proceedings of the Berkeley Linguistics Society, Berkeley, CA.

(1988) "The Split Morphology Hypothesis: Evidence from Yiddish." In *Theoretical Morphology: Approaches in Modern Linguistics*, ed. Michael Hammond and Michael Noonan, 79–100. San Diego, CA: Academic Press.

Pesetsky, David (1985) "Morphology and Logical Form." *Linguistic Inquiry* 16, no. 2: 193–246.

Pollock, Jean-Yves (1989) "Verb Movement, Universal Grammar, and the Structure of IP." *Linguistic Inquiry* 20, no. 3: 365–424.

Poulos, George (1990) *A Linguistic Analysis of Venda*. Pretoria: Via Afrika Ltd.

Ravin, Yael (1990) *Lexical Semantics without Thematic Roles*. Oxford: Clarendon Press.

Reinhart, Tanya (1983) *Anaphora and Semantic Interpretation*. Chicago: University of Chicago Press.

Reinholtz, Charlotte (1999) "On the Characterization of Discontinuous Constituents: Evidence from Swampy Cree." *International Journal of American Linguistics* 65, no. 2: 201–227.

Reynolds, Karl H., and Carol M. Eastman (1989) "Morphologically Based Agreement in Swahili." *Studies in African Linguistics* 20, no. 1: 63–77.

Roberge, Yves (1990) *The Syntactic Recoverability of Null Arguments*. Kingston, Ont., and Montreal: McGill-Queen's University Press.

Ross, John Robert (1967) "Constraints on Variables in Syntax." Doctoral dissertation, Massachusetts Institute of Technology.

Rubanza, Yunus Ismail (1988) "Linear Order in Haya Verbal Morphology: Theoretical Implications." Doctoral dissertation, Michigan State University.

Rugemalira, Josephat M. (1991) "What is a Symmetrical Language? Multiple Object Constructions in Bantu." Paper delivered at the Special Session on African Language Structures, Berkeley, CA.

(1993a) "Bantu 'Multiple Object' Constructions." *Linguistic Analysis* 23, no. 3–4: 226–252.

(1993b) "Runyambo Verb Extensions and Constraints on Predicate Structure." Doctoral dissertation, University of California at Berkeley.

Russell, Kevin, and Charlotte Reinholtz (1996) "Nonconfigurationality and the Syntax-Phonology Interface." Paper delivered at the West Coast Conference on Formal Linguistics.

Sabimana, Firmard (1986) "The Relational Structure of the Kirundi Verb." Doctoral dissertation, Indiana University.

Sadler, Louisa, and Andrew Spencer (1998) "Morphology and Argument Structure." In *The Handbook of Morphology*, ed. Andrew Spencer and Arnold Zwicky, 206–236. Oxford: Blackwell.

Satyo, Sizwe C. (1985) "Topics in Xhosa Verbal Extensions." Doctoral dissertation, University of South Africa, Pretoria, South Africa.

Seidl, Amanda, and Alexis Dimitriadis (2003) "Statives and Reciprocal Morphology in Swahili." In *Typologie des langues d'Afrique et universaux de la grammaire: approches transversales et domaine bantou*, ed. P. Sauzet and A. Zribi-Hertz, 239–284. Paris: L'Harmattan.

Sells, Peter (1984) "Syntax and Semantics of Resumptive Pronouns." Doctoral dissertation, University of Massachusetts, Amherst.

(1985) *Lectures on Contemporary Syntactic Theories*. Stanford, CA: Center for the Study of Language and Information.

Sells, Peter, Annie Zaenen, and Draga Zec (1987) "Reflexivization Variation: Relations between Syntax, Semantics, and Lexical Structure." In *Working Papers in Grammatical Theory and Discourse Structure. Interactions of Morphology, Syntax, and Discourse*, ed. Masayo Iida, Stephen Wechsler, and Draga Zec, 169–238. Stanford, CA: CSLI Publications.

Sibanda, Galen (2004) "Verbal Phonology and Morphology of Ndebele." Doctoral dissertation, University of California, Berkeley.

Simango, Ron (1995) "The Syntax of Bantu Double Object Constructions." Doctoral dissertation, University of South Carolina.

(1999) "Lexical and Syntactic Causatives in Bantu." *Linguistic Analysis* 19, no. 1–2: 69–86.

Speas, Margaret J. (1990) *Phrase Structure in Natural Language* Dordrecht: Kluwer Academic Publishers.

Sproat, Richard (1988) "Bracketing Paradoxes, Cliticization and Other Topics: The Mapping between Syntactic and Phonological Structure." In *Morphology and Modularity*, ed. M. Everaert et al., 339–360. Dordrecht: Foris.

Thomas-Ruzic, Maria (1990) "Passives and Voice in Kikamba." Paper delivered at the 21st African Linguistics Conference, University of Georgia, Athens, GA.

Thwala, Nhlanhla (1995) "A Generative Grammar of SiSwati: The Morphology and Syntax of Nouns and Verbs." Doctoral dissertation, University of California at Los Angeles.

Torrego, Esther (1998) *The Dependencies of Objects*. Linguistic Inquiry Monographs 34, ed. Samuel Jay Keyser. Cambridge, MA: MIT Press.

Travis, Lisa (1984) "Parameters and Effects of Word Order." Doctoral dissertation, Massachusetts Institute of Technology.

Trithart, Lee (1983) "The Applied Affix and Transitivity: A Historical Study in Bantu." Doctoral dissertation, University of California at Los Angeles.

van der Spuy, Andrew (1989) "A Reconstruction of the Phonology of Proto-Southern Bantu." MA thesis, University of South Africa, Pretoria.

Watkins, Mark Hanna (1937) *A Grammar of Chichewa: A Bantu Language Spoken in British Central Africa*. Philadelphia, PA: Linguistic Society of America.

Watters, John R. (1989) "Bantoid Overview." In *The Niger-Congo Languages: A Classification and Description of Africa's Largest Language Family*, ed. John Bendor-Samuel and Rhonda L. Hartell, 400–420. Lanham, MD: University Press of America.

Williams, Edwin (1981) "Argument Structure and Morphology." *The Linguistic Review* 1: 81–114.

Zingani, Willie T. (1989) *Madzi Akatayika*, rev. edn. Blantyre, Malawi: Dzuka Publishing Co. Ltd.

Index